THE LANGUAGE OF LITERATURE
General Editor: N. F. Blake
Professor of English Language and Linguistics
University of Sheffield

THE LANGUAGE OF LITERATURE
General Editor: N. F. Blake

Published titles

The Language of Shakespeare	N. F. Blake
The Language of Chaucer	David Burnley
The Language of Wordsworth and Coleridge	Frances Austin
The Language of Irish Literature	Loreto Todd
The Language of D. H. Lawrence	Allan Ingram

Further titles are in preparation

Other books by Allan Ingram

Boswell's Creative Gloom
Intricate Laughter in the Satire of Swift and Pope
Joseph Conrad: Selected Literary Criticism and 'The Shadow-Line' (ed.)

THE LANGUAGE OF D.H. LAWRENCE

ALLAN INGRAM
Principal Lecturer in English
Newcastle upon Tyne Polytechnic

St. Martin's Press   New York

© Allan Ingram 1990

All rights reserved. For information, write:
Scholarly and Reference Division,
St. Martin's Press, Inc.,
175 Fifth Avenue, New York, N.Y. 10010

First published in the United States of America in 1990

Printed in Hong Kong

ISBN 0–312–03666–3

Library of Congress Cataloging-in-Publication Data
Ingram, Allan.
The language of D.H. Lawrence / Allan Ingram.
p. cm. —(Language of literature.)
Includes bibliographical references.
ISBN 0–312–03666–3
1. Lawrence, D.H. (David Herbert), 1885–1930—Language.
2. Lawrence, D.H. (David Herbert), 1885–1930—Criticism and
interpretation. I. Title. II. Series.
PR6023.A93Z63194   1990
823′.912—dc20   89–10637
                                                        CIP

Contents

To Sarah and Ruth

Preface

Lawrence was one of the most prolific of modern writers. His work covers fiction, poetry, drama and essays, as well as several volumes of letters. This book is not intended to be an exhaustive description of the language of D.H. Lawrence through all the forms of his writing. It is an introduction to the study of one writer by way of the linguistic resources available to him. This necessarily involves some discussion of the contexts of his writing – for example, of the state of literary language during the first two decades of the twentieth century, of Lawrence's own background, and of his attitudes towards literature and towards society. I have also tried, when looking at specific textual examples, to keep a clear focus on their meaning and significance within the context of the whole work. I have concentrated almost exclusively on Lawrence's fiction, and have therefore largely confined myself to discussion of the language of prose. This has enabled me, however, to spend some time on the language of his letters and of his non-fictional prose. The plays are omitted altogether, but I have made space for one chapter on the language of poetry. I have kept to a minimum the use of linguistic terms. Those that have been essential are clearly explained when they first arise, and their application demonstrated through examples. I have used Penguin editions of Lawrence's writing, but have also been alert to textual changes registered in the Cambridge text.

I am grateful to the many friends, colleagues and students who have helped and stimulated this work through discussion and interest. My thanks are especially due to Annie Bergonzi, Jill Fenwick and Jan Hewitt, all of whom read through my manuscript and provided me with valuable suggestions and invaluable encouragement. Finally, I am grateful to Norman Blake for the opportunity to contribute to this series, and for his interest and help.

Newcastle, 1989   A. S. INGRAM

1 Lawrence's Writing and the Context of Modernism

This is Lawrence writing to a friend from his cottage near St Ives. It is the spring of 1917.

> The weather is very hot and lovely. I go about in a silky shirt you gave me, and a pair of trousers, and nothing else. Today I hae been cutting blackthorn and gorse to make a fence to keep the lambs out of my garden. I loathe lambs, those symbols of Christian meekness. They are the stupidest, most persistent, greediest little beasts in the whole animal kingdom. Really, I suspect Jesus of having had *very little* to do with sheep, that he could call himself the Lamb of God. I would truly rather be the little pig of God, the little pigs are infinitely gayer and more delicate in soul. – My garden is very beautiful, in rows. But the filthy lambs have eaten off my broad beans. The salads are all grown, and the scarlet runners are just ready for the spring. (*Letters*, III, 124)

The most striking characteristics of this description are typical of Lawrence at his best as a writer of fiction. It is lively, it is spontaneous, and above all it is personal. The effect of the passage depends upon a playful mixing of the language and tones of two normally incompatible moods, the conversational and the passionate. We have conventional remarks about the weather followed by the account of Lawrence's appearance and activities. But the tone of 'Today I have been cutting . . . ' is immediately undermined by the violence of his outburst, 'I loathe lambs', by the extension, in a typically Lawrentian fashion, of his own opinions to become an implicit criticism of the entire Christian religion, and by the accumulated weight of the three superlatives, 'stupidest, most persistent, greediest'. When the familiar tone returns with 'Really', it is to introduce a sentence in which Lawrence's criticism of Christianity is made explicit, albeit flippantly. The subsequent introduction of the 'little pigs' is a masterstroke, for not only does it allow the humour of the passage to predominate over the passion, but it also provides a lively picture to be contrasted with the lambs. The pigs, frequently associated with greed, are given the qualities of gaiety and delicacy that are more normally attributed to lambs. What is more, the delicacy of the pigs is then used to add force to Lawrence's thunderous return to 'the filthy lambs', making us understand the word 'Ilthy' not only in a rhetorical sense but also quite literally.

The passage is light-hearted and not intended for critical analysis. It does demonstrate, however, Lawrence's natural feel for language, for its rhythms and the control that rhythm can exert over emotion. His manipulation of his reader's responses, even writing without time for revision, is so sure that we forget the lambs and the strength of Lawrence's feelings against them for two whole sentences while he writes in praise of pigs and in straightforward description of his garden. 'My garden is very beautiful, in rows' recalls the structure of the opening sentence, 'The weather is very hot and lovely', and shares, therefore, in its serenity and stillness, with the added attraction of showing the results of Lawrence's labour in its orderly 'rows'. The impact of the returning lambs in 'But the filthy lambs have eaten off my broad beans' is consequently made more frustrating, more amusing, for their temporary absence from our attention. Lawrence's prose, in fact, in its energy and tonal control, has not only described but emotionally recreated the persistence of the lambs and his own passionate response to them.

Lawrence's vitality as a novelist is the vitality of intense personal commitment. One aspect of this commitment is his alertness to the life that is in people and creatures, his recognition of their nature and individuality, be it a man on a barge or a boy in a classroom, both of whom we find in The Rainbow, be it a stallion, as in St Mawr, or, as here, the lambs in his garden. Each example of life makes its own demands on the linguistic resources of the novelist if it is not to be misrepresented. At the same time Lawrence is also committed to his own emotions and opinions and is ready to write from the energy they provide. He can be certain of their validity for the unashamed reason that *he* feels or thinks in this way. This, above all, is responsible for the sense of spontaneity we experience in reading Lawrence at his best and most characteristic, the sense that the novelist is feeling and thinking this now, this minute, as he writes. Personal opinions and personal emotion, however, make their demands on the writer's control of language and its arrangement if they, too, are not to be distorted in the passage. It is Lawrence's achievement, as I shall argue, that he is able to exploit the resources of language, and to exert control over the intensity of personal commitment, without sacrificing the vitality drawn from strong feelings.

Michael Bell says of Lawrence that the 'personal dimension in his writings frequently gets him into trouble',[1] and it does. A second example from his letters demonstrates Lawrence's capacity for producing deeply offensive material, yet it is written with the same intensity and sense of personal commitment as the lambs letter, and even with something of its conversational casualness. This is from his first letter to the American writer Waldo Frank, whom Lawrence had never met. It is in reply to a letter from Frank. Lawrence talks first about *The Rainbow*, then about the situation in Europe in 1917. This leads him to the subject of purity of thought, which he illustrates by reference to the Gadarene swine, and to his desire to escape to America. (B.W. Huebsch was one of Lawrence's American publishers.)

> I shall come to America. I don't believe in Uncle Samdom, of course. But if the rainbow hangs in the heavens, it hangs over the western continent. I very very very much want to leave Europe, oh, to leave England for ever, and come over to America.
>
> I hear Huebsch is a Jew. Are you a Jew also? The best of Jews is, that they *know* truth from untruth. The worst of them is, that they are rather slave-like, and that almost inevitably, in action, they betray the truth they know, and fawn to the powers that be. But they *know* the truth. Only they must cringe their legs and betray it. The material world dominates them with a base kind of fetish domination. Yet they *know* the truth all the while. Yet they cringe their buttocks to the fetish of Mammon, peeping over their shoulders to see if the truth is watching them,

observing their betrayal. – I have got Jewish friends, whom I am
on the point of forswearing for ever. (*Letters*, III, 144)

After the phraseology of the first paragraph, the 'Uncle Samdon',
the rainbow hanging in the heavens and the almost childlike yearn-
ing ('very very very') to leave Europe and the war, the bluntness of
'I hear Huebsch is a Jew. Are you a Jew also?' is forcefully felt. The
casual tone, too, as if Lawrence is inquiring about Frank's holiday
plans, makes the actual matter of the question more arresting. The
remainder of the paragraph is based on an apparent weighing of
the pros and cons of Jewishness. Lawrence's insistence that Jews
'*know* the truth' places a value on them, and is in keeping with
his belief in the importance of religion and ritual in providing
modern man with spiritual roots. But the language of his main
accusation against the Jews, 'slave-like', 'fawn', 'cringe their legs',
'cringe their buttocks to the fetish of Mammon', 'peeping over
their shoulders', makes it clear from the outset that this is no
real weighing. The judgement has been made already, and we
realise that the force of it must be present in the statement
'I hear Huebsch is a Jew.' The 'best' side of the argument,
in fact, reappearing in similarly structured sentences through
the paragraph ('But they *know* . . . Yet they *know* . . . '), can
finally be seen less as a real factor on behalf of Jews than as
an additional reason for their condemnation. These sentences
become a kind of chorus balancing with their familiar pattern
the passionately visual language of the accusatory sentences, and
providing the appearance of a rational reason for condemning
them: they have betrayed the truth over and over again. The
rather archaic tone of 'forswearing' is the last touch, for it gives
to Lawrence a finality of judgement and at the same time a sense
of spiritual rootedness of his own from the strength of which he
can pronounce his verdict.

My point here is not that Lawrence should be regarded as
irredeemably anti-semitic, for that is not the subject of this book.
It is rather that the same skill in the manipulation of language is
evident both here and in the lamb passage, and in each case the
skill derives from the same qualities of passionate commitment and
spontaneity of expression. In writing to Frank, Lawrence is clearly
writing with feeling, with deep personal conviction, oblivious of
the possibility of giving offence to a man he had never met – or

perhaps even courting that possibility. He is giving the truth as he sees it. He is even giving the truth about Jewishness as he sees it, the nature and individuality of being a Jew, as he sees it. Writing with passionate conviction about lambs, however, gets no one 'into trouble', whereas writing about Jews can do. Frank (whom Lawrence addresses as 'Mr Frank'!) was apparently not offended, for the correspondence continued.

There are a variety of ways in which the personal can be seen to intrude into Lawrence's fiction, distorting in some way, getting him into some kind of trouble, or running counter to his declaration in 'Morality and the Novel' that 'When the novelist puts his thumb in the scale, to pull down the balance to his own predilection, that is immorality' (*Phoenix*, p. 528). To give just a few examples, there is a passage of almost a page in Chapter XI of *The Rainbow* (p. 329) in which Lawrence sets out his own argument against the belief of one of his characters, Anton Skrebensky, in 'the highest good of the community'. There is no attempt to present the arguments through the opinions or example of another character, as there is in other parts of the novel. It is as if Lawrence has become so impatient with his own created character that he cannot wait to answer Skrebensky's beliefs with his own. Again, in *St Mawr* there is a long passage (pp. 76–9) after Rico's fall during which his wife Lou rides for help. As she rides she experiences a vision of the evil that afflicts the world, a vision that only occasionally allows us to remember that it is Lou, and not Lawrence himself, whose mind is being portrayed.

> There it was in socialism and bolshevism: the same evil. But bolshevism made a mess of the outside of life, so turn it down. Try fascism. Fascism would keep the surface of life intact, and carry on the undermining business all the better. All the better sport. Never draw blood. Keep the haemorrhage internal, invisible. (p. 78)

It is perhaps characteristic of visions that they are described in language that is not the normal language of the character who is experiencing them. We are not likely to be convinced, however, if the language used is in the polemical style of the novelist. And again, the character of Birkin in *Women in Love* is, as F.R. Leavis puts it, 'obviously very near to a self-dramatization of Lawrence',[2] and as such is frequently held to be too often a mere mouthpiece for Lawrence's own views.

If the personal is sometimes artistically damaging to Lawrence, though, it is vital to recognise that it is also a source of his greatest strength, not only as a novelist but as a writer of all kinds of literature, from sequences of poems to letters, from short stories to works of travel. No other major English writer of the twentieth century has come close to Lawrence in the range of his writing, or succeeded in remaining so completely individual while practising across a variety of forms. If an output that stretches over many forms can be a sign of a writer's not having found the right one, or even of his following the trends of the day, it can also be evidence of an energy, of a capacity to exploit the different emphases afforded by different forms, and of a personality so alert that each experience, each emotion, becomes material demanding appropriate literary expression.

We can return to Lawrence's lambs for a while, and see how treatment in a different form, novel rather than letter, will allow different features to be found in a common topic.[3] In Chapter VI of *The Rainbow*, 'Anna Victrix', Anna Brangwen is sitting beside her husband, Will, in the little church at Cossethay. She looks up at the 'little stained window' and sees there, set in 'the ruby-coloured glass', the 'familiar yellow figure of the lamb holding the banner'. Lawrence continues:

> She had always liked the little red and yellow window. The lamb, looking very silly and self-conscious, was holding up a forepaw, in the cleft of which was dangerously perched a little flag with a red cross. Very pale yellow, the lamb, with greenish shadows. Since she was a child she had liked this creature, with the same feeling she felt for the little woolly lambs on green legs that the children carried home from the fair every year. She had always liked those toys, and she had the same amused, childish liking for this church lamb. Yet she had always been uneasy about it. She was never sure that this Lamb with a flag did not want to be more than it appeared. So she half mistrusted it, there was a mixture of dislike in her attitude to it. (pp. 159-60)

Will, on the other hand, is observed as 'motionless, timeless, with the faint, bright tension on his face' (p. 160). The most obvious difference between this and Lawrence's letter is that here the feelings are those of a character, not necessarily of Lawrence himself. The surface of the paragraph, however, has as much variety as Lawrence's mixing in his letter of the casual and the passionate, except that here the mix is of more subtly distinguished varieties of language. The impression is created of a character whose mind has settled on one item of her surroundings, the lamb, which is then allowed to lead to the contemplation of a series of memories and emotions while she neglects the real purpose of being in church. A high proportion of the verbs take the pluperfect form ('She had always liked . . . '), which has the effect of pushing the focus of the emotions away from the present of the scene but at the same time of rooting those emotions in a past that stretches back to early childhood. The picture of the children carrying their woolly lambs home from the fair gives visual form to what would otherwise be simply a catalogue of imparted information. The static nature of the scene itself, sitting in a church, imposes constraints, forcing Lawrence to focus on the thoughts of the character rather than on actions, again unlike the activities of the letter. The mixing of verbal forms, pluperfect with past continuous ('The lamb . . . was holding'), provides variety here, as well as implying the continuity in Anna's feelings: she had felt this, she was continuing to feel it. But other features are isolated, separated out from being solely the focus of Anna's attention. The lamb 'looking very silly and self-conscious', because Lawrence has used the present participle rather than the simple past, 'looked', is given a permanence and authority that does not depend on it appearing to Anna as silly and self-conscious. More strikingly, the sentence 'Very pale yellow, the lamb, with greenish shadows' stands out alone with no verbal form at all, as if not dependent on any agent's seeing or thinking it.

When we turn to consider the actual object of Anna's and Lawrence's dislike, we begin to find closer parallels between letter and novel. In both cases more than one kind of lamb is involved in the treatment of the topic – real and symbolic in the letter, and depicted, toy and symbolic in the novel – but each turns out at bottom to have a strong religious significance, even in the letter where the religious side is very much forced in. Anna's uneasiness is clearly based upon a suspicion about interpretation, that 'this Lamb with a flag' might want to be 'more than it appeared', that it might, in other words, represent a range of meaning that was above her and beyond her rather than being simply what it looked like, as the toy lambs of her childhood did. At this point we can see how Lawrence is using a single detail to develop one of the novel's main patterns, the way in which characters relate to, or fail to relate to, the unknown, to that which is vaster and more enduring than themselves. We might recall Tom Brangwen, Anna's adoptive father:

> But during the long February nights with the ewes in labour, looking out from the shelter into the flashing stars, he knew he did not belong to himself. He must admit that he was only fragmentary, something incomplete and subject. There were the stars in the dark heaven travelling, the whole host passing by on some eternal voyage. So he sat small and submissive to the great ordering. (p. 40)

Tom, his wife Lydia, her granddaughter Ursula, all have the capacity to see themselves in the context of the unknown without fighting back, without terror of annihilation. Other characters, like Anton Skrebensky, Uncle Tom Brangwen, Winifred Inger, and Anna, see the unknown as so threatening that they are impelled to resist it, even to deny its existence. In doing so, they deny a large part of themselves, remaining creatures who have turned their backs on the rainbow. So Anna suddenly sees what the lamb means.

> Suddenly it gleamed to her dominant, this lamb with the flag. Suddenly she had a powerful mystic experience, the power of the tradition seized on her, she was transported to another world. And she hated it, resisted it. (p. 160)

The rather sedate language and rhythms of the earlier paragraph, taking their tone from the fact that Anna and Will are in church, have disappeared now, and we have the beginning of a gathering surge of emotional uplift with the promise of 'Suddenly', and again 'Suddenly', the second introducing a sentence of three main clauses, three powerfully impressed stages in the experience. Indeed, the word 'power' itself contributes to the surge, appearing first as an adjective modifying the complement in 'she had a powerful mystic experience', and then being picked up in the following clause and promoted to subject, 'the power of the tradition seized on her'.[4] This naturally builds energy into the structure of the passage, suggesting a rising pattern supported by the vitality of its own elements. Anna, conversely, is demoted from subject in 'she had' to complement in 'seized on her'. Here, of course, mirrored in the language, is the nub of Anna's fear: she is threatened by forces more powerful than herself; her personality, that which is uniquely her, is in danger of being dismissed, as she sees it, as insignificant. And the gathering momentum of the paragraph is suddenly halted by the change in language, by Anna's change to resistance: 'And she hated it, resisted it.' The two main verbs reassert her sense of agency, frustrating the prose rhythms, while the threat of the lamb is reduced by the harsh, concise pronoun, repeated, as if to keep the creature firmly in its place. That Will seems so absorbed by the lamb ('What was he doing? What connexion was there between him and the lamb in the glass?') not only makes the threat more distasteful to Anna, but also reminds us that the fear of possession by another person is one of the root causes of the failure of their marriage at this time.

Naturally, we hardly expect to find such extensive and careful rooting of attitudes within larger patterns when we read a letter to a friend, so the description of the lambs in Cornwall is rightly treated in a far lighter vein. It is nevertheless the case that Lawrence straightaway moves to a religious dimension, as if he, like Anna, resents the capacity of the lamb to symbolise a plane which he feels is somehow a detraction from the way things ought to be. The passage is amusing, and its stylistic devices bring out the 'silly' and the entertaining rather than being concerned with character analysis and integration into a pattern of themes. Lawrence, all the same, has been labouring to set his garden in order. His idea of 'beautiful' is represented by the 'rows' of his vegetables. The lambs in their actual presence are an encroachment on his self-expression just as the qualities they symbolise in the Christian religion are an encroachment on his spiritual personality. So, he is working 'to make a fence' to keep them out. He has to preserve his personality, just as Anna does, whether in the order of his garden, where he builds fences, or in his assessment of what is of spiritual value, where he resists with humour and mockery.

Each form, then, novel and letter, has features which permit the writer to develop different facets of his topic, features like the relation assumed between writer and reader, the implications of this relationship for the kind of language that is appropriate, and, in the case of the novel, the existence of an intermediary, the character, between the emotional attitudes portrayed and the emotional response expected from the reader. At the same time, however, we can acknowledge that one predominant issue underlies Lawrence's writing in these two passages, the threat to personality and the response to that threat. Comparing the two, we realise that the Lawrence whose personality has been asserted in the letter is also the Lawrence who has rendered Anna Brangwen's personality with all the forcefulness and delicacy necessary for her particular situation. Here is one significant measure of his success as a novelist of deep personal convictions. We do not doubt that it is Anna who is feeling these things, even when we know that Lawrence felt something like them himself. The force of his own sense of personality, in other words, has been subjugated to the artistic necessity of allowing proper expression of the force of Anna's. If the passage draws on Lawrence's own feelings, thereby gaining in vitality, it is not at the cost of allowing those feelings to show through. (The letter was actually written some three years later than Lawrence's first draft of *The Rainbow*, but the feelings expressed from St Ives are hardly unique in Lawrence's life, or in his correspondence. What he writes in 1917 is typical of the kind of man he was.)

The distinctiveness and value of Lawrence's writing are clarified if we now consider the relation between his work and that of his most significant contemporaries. Lawrence's era was the period of literary modernism. The techniques developed by such writers as Conrad and Joyce, T.S. Eliot and Ezra Pound, were ones designed far more to disguise or conceal the personality of the author than to reveal it. When Stephen Dedalus speaks of the role of the artist in *A Portrait of the Artist as a Young Man*, it is in terms of the removal of the creator from what he has created.

The artist, like the God of the creation, remains within or behind or beyond or above his handiwork, invisible, refined out of existence, indifferent, paring his fingernails.[5]

The stylistic changes throughout *A Portrait* are adopted in order to reflect, first and foremost, the development of Stephen's mind and of his linguistic sophistication. They also, however, act as a kind of denial of authorship. Joyce himself has disappeared behind the linguistic devices that can tell us all we need to know about Stephen and his way of seeing and thinking. Conrad, too, disappears behind narrative devices, behind narrators like Marlow in *Heart of Darkness* and *Lord Jim*, or behind the opinions and experiences of a constantly changing series of characters, as in *Nostromo*. Henry James, in many ways a more traditional novelist than either Conrad or Joyce, is nevertheless a highly influential practitioner of the art of focusing the experience of the novel not through his own eyes but through those of a central character. Here, for example, is James speaking in the preface to *The Portrait of a Lady* of his conception of the role of his central character, Isabel Archer.

'Place the centre of the subject in the young woman's own consciousness,' I said to myself, 'and you get as interesting and as beautiful a difficulty as you could wish. Stick to *that* – for the centre; put the heaviest weight into *that* scale, which will be so largely the scale of her relation to herself. Make her only interested enough, at the same time, in the things that are not herself, and this relation needn't fear to be too limited.'[6]

When we are brought to judge Isabel, it is because she is judging herself, not because James stands back and tells us, and the evidence we weigh in framing our judgement is evidence that has come to us through her own experience and of which she, too, is in full possession. Personality, where it is an issue – as it is with Isabel, and with Martin Decoud in *Nostromo*, and Doctor Sloper in *Washington Square* – is a matter of the character's relation to him or herself. It is the strengths and shortcomings of personality that are under analysis at the same time as they provide the momentum for the progression of the novel – Isabel's urge for experience, Decoud's political vision,

Sloper's egotism and resistance to his daughter's marriage. Only in D.H. Lawrence, among the major modern novelists, do we find personality in the much larger sense of the vitality and limitations of the author himself, and in his work, if it is an issue, as it is in the case of Anna Brangwen, it is also the driving force that is responsible, and manifestly so, for the existence and shape of the entire work.

To say that personality is under analysis in several significant works of literary modernism is to point to one particularly important factor behind the assumptions of the writers of the early years of the twentieth century. At the heart of each of these works is the writer's sense of the dislocation experienced by the individual when faced with conditions of life in the modern world. This dislocation takes many forms. Most obviously, it is the dislocation of the individual from his society. Thomas Hardy had moved, during his career as a novelist which ended with the publication of *Jude the Obscure* in 1895, further and further away from the possibility of a man or woman of character ever being truly integrated into his or her society. In *The Mayor of Casterbridge*, in *Tess of the D'Urbervilles*, and in *Jude*, his protagonists end their lives isolated or persecuted, unvalued and ignored by the societies they once took for granted. Hardy here is in tune with the attitudes that followed in works of fifteen or twenty years later. Stephen Dedalus, Paul Morel in *Sons and Lovers*, Ursula Brangwen, all find the strength to question society and its values and to take the first steps towards independence and self-reliance, while T.S. Eliot's Prufrock is humiliated and defeated by the society which he sees as an irresistible threat to the coherence of his personality and which is apparently more or less oblivious of his existence.

Dislocation, however, goes deeper into the experience of individuality than this, for writers also perceive the questions that have to be asked concerning the individual's relationship with him or herself. These are questions that are particularly raised in the work of Conrad. Where, he asks over and over again, is identity to be found? Where, when Decoud suffers the isolation of his marooning in *Nostromo*, is the sense of self, the sense of his own solidity as a person, that would keep his personality whole and coherent? How is Jim, in *Lord Jim*, to know any kind of truth about himself as he changes place and identity around the Eastern seas, fleeing from his own shameful reputation? Prufrock, too, in beginning his 'Love Song' with 'Let us go then, you and I', is giving a most direct pointer to the dislocation he feels within himself, and Joyce, with the title *A Portrait of the Artist as a Young Man*, implies in the word 'portrait' a deliberate act of framing by which the self that the 'artist' was once is separated from the self he now is, placed at arm's length, in a different region of knowing.

Indeed, what is involved in this kind of dislocation is a fundamental lack of reliance on the traditional resources by which the individual was once able to know and be sure of his or her own identity. Sense impressions, for example, can reaffirm a sense of identity by their continuity, by their assurance that here is a coherent mind experiencing the same world in much the same way from day to day. But when Prufrock says 'Is it perfume from a dress/That makes me so digress?' his experience of the sense of smell confirms for him nothing reliable. It confirms only the unpredictable, even anarchic, tendencies of the human mind. The role of language, too, in the process of identifying oneself is also found to be fundamentally unreliable. If literary language takes its form, as it does in *Portrait of the Artist*, from the stage of development of the protagonist of the work, or from his state of mind, as is the case in *Prufrock*, then it inevitably shares the limitations of his understanding, his views, his capacity for language use. The implication is that language can never be wholly under the control of the user. The user will always remain within his own language, never able to stand outside, as it were, and contemplate his deepest linguistic assumptions. So little is the user in control of his language that he will often be unaware how far his perceptions of the world, his understanding of his own feelings, are governed by the very language he uses to try to make sense of them. That which is capable of being expressed by the individual is in theory limitless, but in practice there will never be a language user able to transcend his or her own limitations in order to exploit linguistic forms to the full. As Eliot puts it in *Four Quartets*,

> That was one way of putting it – not very satisfactory:
> A periphrastic study in a worn-out poetical fashion,
> Leaving one still with the intolerable wrestle
> With words and meanings.[7]

Naturally, this position poses problems for the serious writer. How, after all, can communication be possible, or the attaining of any real knowledge be possible, if language itself is untrustworthy? And how is literature possible? 'We had the experience', says Eliot, 'but missed the meaning.'[8] How is meaning possible if the language we use can never be a reliable tool? Any attempt to capture meaning can only leave us with 'hints and guesses,/Hints followed by guesses'.[9]

Jacob Korg, looking for an underlying source for the Anglo-American literary revolution of the early decades of the twentieth century, has this to say:

> a plausible one, I believe, is to be found in the conviction that the revolutionary writers shared with such neo-idealistic philosophers as F. H. Bradley, Henri Bergson and Ernst Cassirer: that man, his universe and the reality he inhabits are largely products of his own conceptual activities, and that the nature of his experience is strongly controlled by the resources he uses for making it available to consciousness.[10]

For Korg, these 'resources' are language and the uses made of it by the 'revolutionary writers', among whom he includes Joyce, Eliot and Pound, but not Lawrence. But Korg also goes a step further, for this recognition of the nature of our relation to our own language is by no means wholly negative. Were this the case then works like *Portrait of the Artist*, *Ulysses* and *The Waste Land* would today be only museum pieces. For Korg, the recognition was a liberation as much as an imposing of new limitations on the creative writer. He continues:

> The revolt against literary convention is linked to a general sense that art, literature, and, in fact, all forms of knowledge and expression contain radically creative energies which cannot avoid shaping the material they deal with, and must not be allowed to operate in darkness, or fall prey to obsolete motivations.[11]

In other words, the awareness of the shortcomings of our relation to our language opens up the possibility of exploiting those very limitations in the exploration of the individual and his experience. It is precisely his limitations that make him individual. The limitations are no longer something to be overcome, they are at the very centre of the writer's attention, and the challenge is now to render authentically not a sense of the wholeness of vision but of its partiality.

Language, then, and literary form in general, are fields for experiment by modernist writers, aware that the proper expression of a character's seeing is an expression of the how as well as the what of the act of having seen. In the shifting stylistic forms of *Portrait of the Artist*, the restlessness of 'Prufrock', the fragmentariness of *The Waste Land*, and in the multiple, and therefore mutually questioning, viewpoints of *Nostromo*, we see the forms of language and the forms of literature adapting to incorporate the expression of uncertainty, of lack of self-awareness, of fundamental doubts about meaning or the possibility of meaning, of all those aspects which traditional forms were judged to have left 'in darkness'. Where form had traditionally been a model representing a superior level of reality, as conveyed by Keats' use of the Grecian urn against which he measures the imperfections of the actual world, or by the blank verse of Milton or Wordsworth, or by Pope's heroic couplets, we now find it denying any superior level, or at best affirming it only by its absence. The protagonist of *The Waste Land* may be aware of something having been lost, but it is loss that is the focus of the poem, and which is expressed by the poem's form, rather than the wholeness of what once was. He and we see the 'heap of broken images', the 'Sunlight on a broken column' of *The Hollow Men*.[12] If the possibility of wholeness is implied, it is because the poem or novel itself is so suggestive of lack of wholeness.

There is one sense, however, in all experimental or innovatory art in which wholeness, or order, is strongly implied, not through the work's manifestation of the opposite, but through our perception of the role of the artist. When Stephen Dedalus speaks of the artist's detachment, and when we read Joyce's *Portrait*, or Eliot, or Conrad, we are frequently left not with a sense of the work's existing in its own right without the intrusive presence of its author, but rather with a strong impression of having been experimented upon by an intelligence that chooses to remain hidden. In Korg's words, the observer, or reader, 'feels that he is himself being judged by some enigmatic intelligence, some representative of a world of values to which he is a stranger'.[13] We tend to assume not that there is only disorder, but that the disorder we *do* see is in fact the manifestation of an order we do not *yet* see. The extent to which once 'difficult' works are now accepted without question into the canon of English literature suggests that we are perhaps getting better at seeing order. It also suggests that contemporary writers are having to find ever more ingenious ways of disguising it.

Here we have one of the paradoxes of literary modernism. The more a writer labours to achieve impersonality, to refine himself out of existence, the more likely his reader is to identify the personality of the author as a manipulative intelligence playing games with words, the true 'God' of his literary creation. And the more the writer makes his work reflect the dislocation he sees at the heart of modern life, the more likely it is that we shall look for an order organising the disorder. What is more, we shall locate the source of that order in the assumed intentions of the godlike author, the 'representative of a world of values' to which we and our kind are strangers. He will be found in every choice he has made, from the choice between novel and poem, between comedy and contemplation, one narrator and several, long sentences and short, one word rather than another. It is not in human nature to rest easily in the assumption that there is no one there!

I have spent some time on literary modernism because it allows us to focus with greater clarity on what is different about Lawrence, as well as on what he has in common with his leading contemporaries. He certainly shared their perception of the dislocations experienced by the individual in the modern world, and analysed them with growing impatience as his own disgust with twentieth-century life increased. He was also convinced of the necessity for new attitudes in the writer, towards character, towards literary form, and towards language, if the modern condition was to be properly portrayed. These topics will be pursued in subsequent chapters. Where Lawrence differs, and markedly so, from writers like Conrad, Joyce and Eliot, is in the level of his seriousness.

It is no doubt strange to suggest that the authors of *Heart of Darkness* and *Ash Wednesday* lacked seriousness. There is in both, however, and especially in James Joyce, a strong element of playfulness with form and language that is not found in Lawrence. This is not to say that Eliot is not in earnest in the contemplation of his, or his speaker's, spiritual condition, and in his desire for redemption. There is nevertheless a quite separate pleasure in reading *Ash Wednesday* that resides in our perception of Eliot's manipulation of poetic devices, including, of course, his exploitation of such models as Dante and the Bible. The very fact that we are unsure whether it is Eliot's soul or the speaker of the poem's is evidence of the two levels of response that the poem produces. With Lawrence, there is no playfulness. We can, of course, admire the form of *The Rainbow*, and admire it at a different level from our engagement with its contents. But the admiration is never at odds with the engagement, because the distinctive character of the work is the same in each aspect. There is no playful manipulativeness to set against earnestness. Instead, there are mistakes, which is simply another way of acknowledging seriousness. There is personality, the force of which leaves no room for games with language. For Lawrence, language is there to convey what needs to be conveyed, not to be contemplated and enjoyed as a field of play. If it can tell us nothing about ourselves, then it is of no interest to him. As Michael Bell puts it, 'Lawrence's usage is, we might say, entirely within the skin of the language'.[14]

There is a very obvious reason for this difference. Lawrence was a writer with a strong sense of mission. He saw the falsities and sickness of modern life and saw, too, that the way for him to try to change people was through writing. As he says to his friend McLeod in 1913, 'I do write because I want folk – English folk – to alter, and have more sense' (*Letters*, I, 544). Modern art, according to Octavio Paz, 'is modern because it is critical'.[15] If Lawrence is critical, he is also a positive writer in that he offers, and offers with the force of conviction, ways out of our emotional and spiritual dilemmas. We may from time to time feel that Lawrence's positive force is responsible for an over-assertiveness in doctrine, and for shrill or hectoring language. But what we never find is emotional laziness, a reliance on technique rather than feeling, what Bell calls 'the covert assumption . . . that the technical resolution guarantees the spiritual one'. Bell continues:

> The whole question of 'impersonality', for example, that particularly exercised Joyce and Eliot, became for them a self-conscious and technical affair sometimes doing duty for,

and even precluding, the actual impersonality of emotional acceptance that comes through the highly personal voices of Lawrence, Dostoevsky or Dickens when those writers are actually doing their job.[16]

In the following chapters I shall be discussing Lawrence's background, his attitudes towards writing and to the novel in particular, his conception of character and his treatment of relationships and of the fictional world in which they take place. In all of these things I shall be concentrating on what they tell us about his attitudes towards language, and looking closely at how he used it. For it is in his language, first and foremost, that Lawrence or any writer can be seen to be doing his job.

2 Lawrence's Early Life

In his autobiographical work, *Return to Yesterday*, published in 1931, Ford Madox Ford describes a visit to Lawrence at his family's home in Eastwood. The visit would have taken place during the spring of 1912, while Lawrence was convalescing after the pneumonia that led him to resign his teaching post in Croydon. In March of that year he met Frieda Weekley, the wife of his former Professor of French at University College, Nottingham, and on 3 May Lawrence and Frieda eloped together to Germany. This is what Ford says he found:

I visited him in Nottingham and was astonished at the atmosphere in which he lived though less astonished by then as to the great sense of culture in his work. Lawrence's father, of French extraction and great force of character, was a buttyman down the mine and one of his brothers also worked underground. His sister I think was, like Lawrence, a school teacher. Other young people from down the pit or from schools and offices drifted in and out of the Lawrences' house with the sort of freedom from restraint that I have only seen elsewhere in American small towns. I have never anywhere found so educated a society. Those young people *knew* the things that my generation in the great English schools hardly even chattered about. Lawrence, the father, came in from down the mine on a Saturday evening. He threw a great number of coins on the kitchen table and counted them out to his waiting mates. All the while the young people were talking about Nietzsche and Wagner and Leopardi and Flaubert and Karl Marx and Darwin and occasionally the father would interrupt his counting to contradict them. And they would discuss the French Impressionists and the primitive Italians and play Chopin or Debussy on the piano.

> I went with them on the Sunday to a non-conformist place of worship. . . . The Nottingham chapel – it was I think Wesleyan – made me of course feel uncomfortable at first. But the sermon renewed my astonishment. It was almost entirely about – Nietzsche, Wagner, Leopardi, Karl Marx, Darwin, the French Impressionists and the primitive Italians. I asked one of Lawrence's friends if that was not an unusual sort of sermon. He looked at me with a sort of grim incredulity.
>
> "What do you suppose? he said. "Do you think we would sit under that fellow if he could not preach like that for fifty-two Sundays a year? He would lose his job."[1]

There is, in fact, no certainty that Ford ever did visit Lawrence. Edward Nehls, who included the passage in *D.H. Lawrence: A Composite Biography*, expresses doubt, and adds that 'Mr. Douglas Goldring, an authority on Ford, has written in a letter to the editor (16 September 1955) that he now regards Ford's claim as "'fanciful,' like so many of Ford's claims".' And Harry T. Moore describes the idea as 'incredible' and 'extremely fantastic'.[2] Nevertheless, factual or fanciful, the description conveys the forces that had been at work shaping the development of Lawrence's mind through the early years of his life: the family circle, voracious and largely unsystematic reading, and non-conformist religion. All of these factors contribute towards his literary attitudes and towards the texture of his writing, and while the contribution is inevitably clearest in the early novels, *The White Peacock*, *The Trespasser* and *Sons and Lovers*, we find it still in various forms influencing the conception and expression of his last novels and stories.

Yet there is one early influence on Lawrence that Ford does not describe. Lydia Lawrence had died in December 1910. As every account of Lawrence's life makes clear, including his own in *Sons and Lovers* and Jessie Chambers' in *D.H. Lawrence: A Personal Record*, his mother was the single most important person in his emotional and mental development. Ada, Lawrence's younger sister, describes her and something of her influence on the household.

She was small and slight in figure, her brown hair sprinkled with grey, brushed straight back from a broad brow; clear blue eyes that always looked fearless and unfaltering, and a delicately shaped nose, not quite straight owing to an accident which occurred when she was a girl; tiny hands and feet, and a sure carriage. Some people were ill-natured enough to say that she "put it on" when she spoke, for her English was good and her accent so different from that of the folk round about.

Try as she might, she could never speak the local dialect, and we children were careful about it when we were with her, even though we let fling among our friends. She loved to read, and every week piles of books were fetched from the local library to be enjoyed when we were all in bed. The minister liked to visit her, and they discussed religion and philosophy, for she was an excellent talker, and had a dry, whimsical, fascinating sense of humour. She was never effusive or demonstrative in any way, yet we felt in her a wealth of love and a security past all understanding. (Nehls, p. 9)

If we see here the strength of character and sense of superiority that go into Mrs Morel in *Sons and Lovers*, we see also something of the self-contained confidence and capacity for love of Lydia Lensky in *The Rainbow*. In the personality of Mrs Lawrence attitudes towards language and towards learning are focused and given emotional resonance. The home is where one speaks with care, rather than 'letting fling' as when with friends, yet at the same time love and security are found under the influence of the woman who, as Lawrence also puts it, 'spoke King's English, without an accent, and never in her life could even imitate a sentence of the dialect which my father spoke, and which we children spoke out of doors' (*Phoenix II*, p. 592). What in Mrs Morel is treated as class consciousness, however, becomes in Lydia Lensky an inevitable feature of her foreignness and so part of the fascination felt for her by Tom Brangwen: what was a feature of separateness in *Sons and Lovers* has been turned to one of attraction in *The Rainbow*. Yet in both works, the mother is not only a source of love and security but of the desire for her children to better themselves. Where Mrs Morel encourages reading and education, in *The Rainbow* it is not specifically Lydia but the women in general who, over succeeding generations, look out 'from the heated, blind intercourse of farm-life, to the spoken world beyond', to education, to the vicar, and to the 'magic language' of fulfilment (*Rainbow*, pp. 8–9).

Yet Ada has another point to make concerning the influence of Lydia Lawrence within the home.

> I wonder if there would have been quite so much misery in our childhood if mother had been just a little more tolerant. Having been brought up in a strict and puritanical atmosphere, she was a staunch teetotaller, and would have no strong drink in the house. My father, who had received little education, being sent to work when he was seven, felt no desire to read anything but newspapers. Having little in common with mother, he soon began to seek the more congenial society of his friends in the public-house, not solely for the sake of drink, but because in their company he was more sure of himself, and their interests were his interests. (Nehls, p. 10)

Here the emphasis is exclusively on separateness, on class consciousness and on the differences in moral values and outlook that accompany differences in linguistic awareness and language use. Lawrence rather grudgingly says, 'My mother was, I suppose, superior' (*Phoenix II*, p. 592). His emotional ambivalence seems to surface when he makes Paul Morel, a speaker of 'King's English', adopt dialect for some of his more tender scenes with Clara Dawes, or when Mellors, in *Lady Chatterley's Lover*, is made to drop standard English in favour of dialect once the love relationship with Connie is under way. It is as if the love and security associated with home are damaged by the care required to speak well. For true intimacy, relaxation from class consciousness and from sexual separateness is afforded by dialect.

For Lawrence, though, separation between the sexes seems to remain as a fact of life, albeit one disguised by education. If his novels frequently show sexual warfare breaking out in spite of the veneer of civilisation, as it does between Ursula and Anton in *The Rainbow*, or between Gudrun and Gerald in *Women in Love*, he also observes the natural tendency, especially in peasant life, of the sexes to remain irrevocably apart, even in marriage. Paolo and Maria are host and hostess at San Gaudenzio.

> With regard to Maria, Paolo omitted himself; Maria omitted herself with regard to Paolo. Their souls were silent and

detached, completely apart, and silent, quite silent. They shared the physical relationship of marriage as if it were something beyond them, a third thing. (*Twilight in Italy*, p. 92)

Separateness here is not even concentrated in difference in language. It is a matter of silence, beyond expression, like the silence of the courting couple in Lawrence's poem, 'Sunday Afternoon in Italy', who walk 'With an interval of space between'. The walk over, 'he sighs with relief' as she leaves him, and he goes, like John Lawrence and Walter Morel, to 'join/The men that lounge in a group on the wharf'.

> His evening is a flame of wine
> Among the eager, cordial men.
> And she with her women hot and hard
> Moves at her ease again.
>
> (*Complete Poems*, I, 228)

The influence of Lydia on Lawrence's attitude towards language is profound and complex, for in her example are combined love and separateness, security and class consciousness, learning and sexual warfare. At the same time, like the women of *The Rainbow*, her desire for and encouragement of learning are inseparable from her attachment to religion and the institutions of the church or, in the Lawrences' case, the non-conformist chapel. Not only did the minister visit for religious and philosophical discussion but, as Emile Delavenay describes,

> Regular attendance at religious service was expected from all and formed part of the system by which the children were to raise themselves to a superior level, thus bettering their social rank. So three times every Sunday they would go to chapel, attending morning and evening service, and in the afternoon a Sunday School.[3]

The language of learning, therefore, is the language of the Bible, of hymns, and of Congregationalist teaching. In 'Hymns in a Man's Life' Lawrence testifies to the power of 'the hymns which I learned as a child, and never forgot. They mean to me

almost more than the finest poetry, and they have for me a
more permanent value, somehow or other' (*Phoenix II*, p. 597).
Lawrence had, as he claimed, 'got over the Christian dogma' by
the time he was sixteen (*Phoenix II*, p. 599), and even wrote
an incompetent Congregationalist minister into *Paul Morel*, the
first version of *Sons and Lovers*. Nevertheless the language and
rhythms of the Bible are everywhere in his prose (the prevalence
of short sentences beginning 'And', and the reliance upon patterns
of repetition, are the most obvious examples), and the expression
natural to temperance tracts gets into *Sons and Lovers* in sentences
like 'She knew that the man who stops on the way home from work
is on a quick way to ruining himself and his home'.[4] And while
Lawrence's poetry is most characterised by freedom and irregu-
larity, the strong, 'rather banal' (*Phoenix II*, p. 597) rhythms of
the Bristol hymn-book occasionally slip into verses of poems, as
in 'A Young Wife':

> The pain of loving you
> Is almost more than I can bear. . . .
>
> Now every tall glad tree
> Turns round its back to the sun
> And looks down on the ground, to see
> The shadow it used to shun.
>
> (*Complete Poems*, I, 215)

Just as the creation of Lydia Lensky is, in one sense, a tribute to
Lydia Lawrence's capacity for real love, and therefore a version
of what might have been, so here the language that speaks of
love between man and woman takes tone and rhythm from the
religious love to which Mrs Lawrence turned and from the hymns
which were its most fervent expression.

By no means all of Lawrence's childhood reading was religious
or conducted under the guidance of Congregationalism. Among
his earliest literary pleasures were the adventure stories and tales
– *Coral Island*, *Swiss Family Robinson*, or *Little Folks* – told
to the younger children, as Ada records, by their sister Emily
(Nehls, p. 13). He also, apparently, enjoyed Frederick Marryat

and James Fenimore Cooper (Delavenay, p. 10). But it was during his adolescent years, and especially with the growth of the intimacy with Jessie Chambers, that Lawrence's reading begins to be well documented. It is marked by voraciousness and a high degree of imaginative involvement. Jessie records Lawrence bringing a first book to her – *Little Women* – and adds, 'We thought the story delightful, and set about finding correspondences. I was Jo, there was no doubt about that, and Lawrence was Laurie.' There was the set of books, 'large volumes bound in green cloth containing long extracts from famous authors', that had belonged to Ernest Lawrence, the dead elder brother (William of *Sons and Lovers*) and 'were regarded with a reverence amounting to awe'. And Lawrence and Jessie would go weekly to the library of the Eastwood Mechanics' Institute.

> Then Lawrence and I would set off for my home literally bur-
> dened with books. During the walk we discussed what we had
> read last, but our discussion was not exactly criticism, indeed it
> was not criticism at all, but a vivid re-creation of the substance
> of our reading. Lawrence would ask me in his abrupt way what
> I thought of such and such a character, and we would compare
> notes and talk out our differences. The characters interested us
> most, and there was usually a more or less unconscious identi-
> fication of them with ourselves, so that our reading became a
> kind of personal experience.[5]

An example of this kind of 'criticism' is when they read *Coriolanus*:

> One afternoon he came up with his volume of Shakespeare
> under his arm and we sat down and read *Coriolanus* straight
> away. I wondered at his look of puzzled concentration, and
> felt that the play had a significance for him that I had not
> grasped.
> 'You see, it's the mother who counts,' he said, 'the wife
> hardly at all. The mother is everything to him.' (Chambers,
> pp. 61–2)[6]

During this period, the years between 1901, when Lawrence was fifteen, and 1908, when he left to teach in Croydon and the intimacy with Jessie began to wane, the list of reading includes

Dickens, George Eliot, R.L. Stevenson, Anthony Hope, Victor Hugo, Maupassant, Tolstoy, Flaubert, Gissing, Poe and Balzac in prose, Longfellow, Blake, Tennyson, Petrarch, Shelley, Rossetti, Thomas Hood, Pope, Verlaine, Baudelaire, Coleridge and Spenser in poetry. In addition, there are writers of non-fictional prose, including Swift, Bacon, Darwin, De Quincy, Locke, Emerson, Lamb, T.H. Huxley, William James, Mill, Herbert Spencer, Diderot, Hegel, Hume, Lessing and Nietzsche.[7] Many of these, after 1906, were read as part of Lawrence's degree course at the university college, but many more were read and discussed with Jessie.

Two particularly significant features emerge from Lawrence's early reading. One is its context, the other its application. First with his mother and his immediate family, especially the female members of it, then with Jessie, literature is experienced as part of a warm and secure relationship, as an element within the relationship and one that seems to strengthen and give meaning to it. Lawrence was always vehement against any kind of reading – or writing – that fostered an attitude of sterility. He detested working for his London Matriculation Examination, and wrote to Jessie 'of the misery of "pen-driving in the city heat" '. Or, on school practice, he condemned the essay work as 'sheer imitation' and the 'absolute ruin of their spontaneous expression'. The 'main purpose of education', he told Jessie, 'was to teach people how to use their leisure, or rather how to use themselves' (Chambers, pp. 75, 80). Reading, as it developed during Lawrence's early years, was not a solitary pursuit but one that necessarily involved a response shared between two or more individuals within a relationship of trust and affection. Literary language, therefore, was a medium that stimulated and flowed into the spoken language of mutual exploration and personal awareness. In a context in which reading and its discussion are regarded as shared 'personal experience', the language of literature is that which engages imaginative involvement and best enables readers 'to use themselves'.

These attitudes, naturally enough, govern Lawrence's expectations of his own early writing. He requires the warmth of a secure relationship in which his work can be received and discussed, and the writing itself, like the shared reading, is a vital part of the relationship. Jessie was the first partner, and probably in this respect the most important.

Lawrence was constantly bringing his writing to me, and I always had to tell him what I thought of it. He would ask whether the characters had developed, and whether the conversation was natural, if it was what people really would say. He found conversation easy and wondered if it was too easy. He feared he had a tendency towards verbosity; perhaps he ought to condense his writing more. . . . He always declared that he did the writing for me.

'Every bit I do is for you,' he said. 'Whenever I've done a fresh bit I think to myself: What will she say to this? ' And of his poetry he said, 'All my poetry belongs to you.' (Chambers, pp. 115–16)

Appropriately, Lawrence's earliest published piece, the short story 'A Prelude' (variously called 'A Prelude to a Happy Christmas' and 'An Enjoyable Christmas. A Prelude'), which won a £3 prize in the *Nottinghamshire Guardian* Christmas competition for 1907, was submitted under Jessie's name. (The second of the three stories submitted by Lawrence, 'The White Stocking', this time under the name of Louie Burrows, to whom he was to become engaged in 1910, is an idealised picture of his mother as a young girl at a Christmas ball.) It was Jessie, too, who, in 1909, sent to Ford Madox Ford at the *English Review* the poems that achieved for Lawrence his first serious literary publication.

By Christmas 1907, Lawrence had already been working on his first novel, *The White Peacock* (then called 'Laetitia'), for eighteen months, and was now in the middle of the second version. Like everything else, it was written with Jessie in mind, even during the final rewriting at Croydon in 1909 when their relationship was in its last stages.

I had not a high opinion of the first version of *The White Peacock*, in which George married Letty. . . . The novel, apart from its setting, seemed to me story-bookish and unreal. . . . Yet in spite of its sentimentality, a thread of genuine romance ran through the story; something in the atmosphere was alive. . . .

In the second writing the story was radically altered and the characters became more like flesh and blood, except Cyril, who remained as he began, old-maidish. Lawrence concentrated upon George, and the figure of Annable emerged, at first only cynically brutal, but later developing into symbolic stature. I was horrified at Annable's first appearance and remonstrated with Lawrence, but he shook his head decisively, and said:

'He *has* to be there. Don't you see why? He makes a sort of balance. Otherwise it's too much one thing, too much *me*,' and grinned. . . .

The rounding-off of the story Lawrence wrote during our brief moment of harmony. He said in a letter: 'Do you mind if, *in the novel*, I make Emily marry Tom?' I didn't mind in the least. I thought the final turn one of the happiest human touches in the book. (Chambers, pp. 116–19)

Other people, however, also influenced the writing and rewriting of *The White Peacock*, not least Mrs Lawrence, whose first reaction, according to Jessie, was one of revulsion from the marriage of the middle-class Letty to George, the sturdy yeoman.

I think Lawrence despised the story from the bottom of his heart, for he immediately started to rewrite it. He must have shown it to his mother because when we were on holiday at Robin Hood's Bay I asked her what she thought of it, and she replied, in a pained voice:

'To think that *my* son should have written such a story,' referring presumably to Letty's situation. (Chambers, p. 117)

Such a comment is some confirmation of Ford's later suggestion that 'Lawrence considered himself rather shudderingly as the product of a martyred lady-saint and a savage lower-class father' and that 'he oriented his thoughts and his character along the lines that would be approved by his mother and those in similar circumstances' (Nehls, p. 115). William Edward Hopkin, too, who knew Lawrence in his Eastwood and Croydon days, has testified to 'the profound influence his mother had on his whole life. She dominated every side of it, and her one desire was to see him become a great writer. . . . When he was writing *The White Peacock*, he and his mother criticised it together, and he rewrote parts of it until it satisfied them.' (Nehls, p. 72) Helen Corke, a teacher friend with whom Lawrence became deeply involved in

Croydon, and Ford Madox Ford, too, both contributed to the
revising of this first novel, while his close friend, Alice Dax, and
Blanche Jennings, a suffragist whom he met at Mrs Dax's house
and thereafter corresponded with, were given early versions of
the book for comment.

This writing by committee attitude, as Lawrence consults first
those people who appear in the story, then outsiders, is reflected
in the lack of coherence of even the published text of *The White
Peacock*. On the one side we have those themes and figures that
Lawrence was to return to again and again in his more mature
fiction, of love across social classes, of the strengths and constraints
of life in a working-class environment, and men of powerful
animal instinct, like Annable, or torn by frustrated emotion,
like George. On the other we have the artificiality of much of
the conversation, the spiritless detachment of the narrator, and
the elevating of the Beardsall family's social position away from
the realities of Lawrence's own past, as if in deference to Mrs
Lawrence's offended sensibilities and in tribute to her aspirations
and character. (Beardsall was actually Mrs Lawrence's maiden
name.) We know, from Jessie Chambers, that Lawrence's favour-
ite reading over the long period of writing this novel included
George Moore's *Esther Waters*, Balzac's *Eugénie Grandet*, Hardy,
Meredith, George Eliot, Emily Brontë, Tennyson, Swinburne and
Rossetti, which results, as Keith Sagar suggests, in the 'too literary,
second-hand' treatment of the situations and characters, and in the
'self-conscious poeticality' of his writing about nature.[8] Neither in
subject matter nor, with a few exceptions, in the use of language,
was Lawrence at this time able to see clearly the focus of what
he was attempting. He was apparently trying to pull together so
many contradictory intentions – not least the wish to satisfy both
his mother and Jessie – that he ends by achieving none of them.
And it is in the language particularly that the strains tell.

Here, for example, is the first paragraph of the novel.

I stood watching the shadowy fish slide through the gloom
of the mill-pond. They were grey, descendants of the silvery
things that had darted away from the monks, in the young
days when the valley was lusty. The whole place was gathered
in the musing of old age. The thick-piled trees on the far shore
were too dark and sober to dally with the sun; the weeds stood

crowded and motionless. Not even a little wind flickered the willows of the islets. The water lay softly, intensely still. Only the thin stream falling through the millrace murmured to itself of the tumult of life which had once quickened the valley.

I was startled into the water from my perch on the alder roots by a voice. . . . (p. 13)[9]

Lawrence's first sentence is effective. He has his eye on the object, and the movement of the fish is suggested with the play of 's' sounds, and of 'i' and 'd', in 'shadowy fish slide'. Moreover, 'stood', which introduces both 's' and 'd', is itself undermined by the slipperiness of the sounds that follow, as the narrator's 'watching' is by the shift in perspective from firm standing to the movement of the fish. However, 'gloom' is probably redundant, as the fish are already 'shadowy', and 'mill-pond' is not quite right as it shifts perspective too abruptly from below the surface of the water to a broader scene that includes by suggestion the mill itself. From here on the writing is ruined by personification, by unruly suggestions, and by conflicting associations. The word 'descendants' is too heavy and dignified coming after the movement of the fish, and the attempt to suggest that these fish are somehow old and 'grey' not only pulls against the effect of their sliding in the first sentence, but is also contrary to common sense: some fish are grey, and some silver, and always have been, and many are as capable of darting now as they were when monks tried to catch them. The 'musing of old age' comes across as fabricated, therefore, and if the verb 'gathered' has some promise, it remains unreleased after the vagueness of 'The whole place'. The next sentence has both uncertainty in meaning – what are 'thick-piled trees', how would they 'dally with the sun', and what are trees like when they are 'sober', or not sober? % and a strained perspective, with the 'far shore' giving an impression of distance that is contradicted by the closeness of 'thick-piled' and 'dark'. 'Not even a little wind' is both an ugly opening to a sentence, even if 'Lickered' gives a genuine sense of willows touched by a breeze (though here, of course, they are not being 'Lickered'), and a clumsy way of asserting stillness by denying that which is only slightly different from it

While 'thin stream' carries the right sound and sight associations, and 'falling through' once again effectively dislodges the stability of the watcher's perspective, their suggestiveness is cut off by the cosy conventionality of 'murmured' and the extraordinary contradiction Lawrence achieves between 'murmured' and 'tumult' when one is supposedly contained within the other. Finally, the narrator's 'perch on the alder roots' not only carries the comic possibility of his being some kind of bird but also makes us reassess our reading of the entire paragraph in the light of his not being, after all, 'stood' at the edge of the mill-pond but rather perched above it.

The lack of ease in the writing, the self-consciousness in diction and placing, the overall lack of judgement, seem attributable to Lawrence's determination to make things mean, rather than being content to let them be themselves first and foremost and only mean once they are properly established. Where the passage is effective it is because the object has been described in a way that is true to itself and at the same time is resonant with realisable potential – the sliding of the 'shadowy fish', the 'thin stream'. Elsewhere, however, intention is too close to the surface of the writing, inhibiting clear-sightedness, creating the impression of an effete and self-conscious narrator/participant, and frustrating the potential of some of the phrasing.

Not all of *The White Peacock* is as strained as this. Written and rewritten as it was over four years it naturally bears the marks of different stages in Lawrence's growing maturity. While the opening was no doubt written over several times, one section which can be dated as a late addition is that dealing with Emily's marriage to Tom for which he sought Jessie's approval, perhaps as late as July 1909 (*Letters*, I, 131 and n. 1). Her judgement of it as 'one of the happiest human touches in the book' is borne out, and particularly so when one looks at the difference in the use of language. Here is Cyril's first visit to Emily's home.

. . . I followed her into the kitchen, catching a glimpse of the glistening pans and the white wood baths as I passed through the scullery. The kitchen was a good-sized, low room that through long course of years had become absolutely a home. The great beams of the ceiling bowed easily, the chimney-seat had a bit of dark-green curtain, and under the high mantelpiece was another low shelf that the men could reach with their hands as they sat in the ingle-nook. There the pipes lay. Many generations of peaceful men and fruitful women had passed through the room, and not one but had added a new small comfort; a chair in the right place, a hook, a stool, a cushion, a certain pleasing cloth for the sofa covers, a shelf of books. The room, that looked so quiet and crude, was a home evolved through generations to fit the large bodies of the men who dwelled in it, and the placid fancy of the women. At last, it had an individuality. It was the home of the Renshaws, warm, lovable, serene. Emily was in perfect accord with its brownness, its shadows, its ease. I, as I sat on the sofa under the window, felt rejected by the kind room. I was distressed with a sense of ephemerality, of pale, erratic fragility. (p. 361)

What is immediately clear is that Cyril is in fact no longer really necessary to Lawrence's rendering of the impression of the scene. Once he has 'passed through the scullery' his presence is superfluous to the descriptive requirements of the writing. Even his 'glimpse' of the pans and the baths is subordinated to the eye-catching detail of what he has glimpsed, 'glistening' and 'white'. And this sets the tone for the paragraph. What is seen is described without the burden of significance. Objects are allowed to stand for themselves, first, and to mean only after the atmosphere has been gradually established. If 'absolutely a home' is a little directed, it is nevertheless unobtrusively stated alongside the commonplace diction of 'a good-sized, low room'. The placing and structure of the sentences are carefully judged. The 'great beams' are balanced in impact by the 'bit of dark-green curtain', and their bowing 'easily' suggests without intrusiveness the gentle settling of the house over the generations. The length of this sentence, with its three main clauses, the third made longer by two subordinate clauses ('that the men could reach . . .' and 'as they sat . . .'), gathers the weight of passing time as it proceeds, yet is held in check by the increasing precision of the focus that moves from the beams to the curtain, to the high then the low shelf, and finally to the imagined hands of the men. This counter-movement is resolved in the short sentence, 'There the pipes lay', when the sharpest focus of all is saved for the object of the reaching hands. With the next long sentence Lawrence is able to include appropriate judgements: the men can be described as 'peaceful' after the serenity of the room has been conveyed, and after the quiet hands feeling for the pipes; the women are 'fruitful' because Emily is herself 'six months gone with child' (p. 361). The picture does not have the depth and range of the opening of *The Rainbow*, but both share a dependence on Lawrence's ability to combine accumulation of time with unfussy observation of the details of everyday life. The simple list of added comforts is both a chronicle of the passing years and an objective description of the smaller features of the room as they would gradually reveal themselves to a new visitor. Only when Cyril reappears as narrator at the end is there a note of jarring, not merely the deliberate note of the intruder, but the jarring of bookish, unfelt diction – the 'sense of ephemerality', the 'pale, erratic fragility'. The language, in short, goes to pieces again. Moreover, the position of the narrator, who had apparently entered into the atmosphere of the room so completely as to let us know it through his impressions, is suddenly shifted and he declares himself completely at odds with it. The awkward self-consciousness of the last sentences – 'I, as I sat on the sofa . . . ' – reflects not so much Cyril's own position as he feels it in the 'kind room', but rather Lawrence's own awkwardness in continuing to write through this self-portrait that was never really himself.

Lawrence sent the second version of *The White Peacock* to Ford in the autumn of 1909, reporting to Louie Burrows that 'He says it's good' (*Letters*, I, 144). In December he wrote to the publisher William Heinemann, to whom Ford recommended the novel, promising 'to fulfil all Mr. Hueffer's injunctions' (*Letters*, I, 149). Ford (Hueffer) himself describes spending 'immensely long sittings' with Lawrence justifying his suggested emendations,

> And sometimes he would accept them and sometimes he wouldn't . . . but always with a great deal of natural sense and without *parti pris*. I mean that he did not stick obstinately to a form of words because it was his form of words, but he required to be convinced before he would make any alterations. (Nehls, pp. 120–1)

The influence Ford had on the texture of Lawrence's writing was apparently one of restraint. This was what Ford particularly valued in his remarks on the opening of the story 'Odour of Chrysanthemums', the first of Lawrence's fiction that he saw: 'He knows the life he is writing about in a landscape just sufficiently constructed with a casual word here and there.' (Nehls, p. 109) Lawrence did not underestimate the debt he owed to Ford, and acknowledged his kindness and encouragement (*Phoenix II*, 593–4), but at the same time seemed to feel stifled by Ford's restraint and by his sense of literary form. He wrote in June 1912 to Walter de la Mare about 'Paul Morel', which he had just sent to Heinemann:

> It's not so strongly concentric as the fashionable folk under French influence – you see I suffered badly from Hueffer re Flaubert and perfection – want it. It may seem loose – and I may cut the childhood part – if you think better so – and perhaps you'll want me to spoil some of the good stuff. But it is rather great. (*Letters*, I, 417)

Ford, who later concluded 'I don't – and I didn't then – think that my influence was any good to him' (Nehls, p. 121), did, however, perform one final invaluable service to Lawrence, and that was to introduce him to Edward Garnett. Garnett was not only reader to the publisher Duckworth, but also a man of discriminating literary judgement and with the capacity to appreciate something startlingly new. His advice had contributed to the success of many writers, not least Joseph Conrad. For Lawrence, his help began with batches of stories and poems, and with *The Trespasser*. But it was with *Sons and Lovers* that his influence became crucial. *Sons and Lovers* is the most significant book of Lawrence's early career, bringing together many facets of his life and writing, and the version that was published by Duckworth in 1913 displays above all the importance of Garnett in shaping the development of Lawrence as a writer.

Lawrence began work on 'Paul Morel' in the autumn of 1910, shortly before the death of his mother, and intended, from the outset, to make it a different style of work altogether from *The White Peacock* and *The Trespasser*: 'Paul Morel will be a novel – not a florid prose poem, or a decorated idyll running to seed in realism: but a restrained, somewhat impersonal novel. It interests me very much.' (*Letters*, I, 184) Jessie, who for a long while did not know of the work, was sent the manuscript of the second version in October 1911, and seems to have found the restraint quite unsatisfactory.

> The whole thing was somehow tied up. The characters were locked together in a frustrating bondage, and there seemed no way out. The writing oppressed me with a sense of strain. It was extremely tired writing. I was sure that Lawrence had had to force himself to do it. The spontaneity that I had come to regard as the distinguishing feature of his writing was quite lacking. (Chambers, p. 190)

Her advice on this occasion was to return to the reality of the story he was telling, and she responded to his subsequent request to 'write what I could remember of our early days' (Chambers, p. 191). This was one of the last services she would render. He would shortly meet Frieda who, with Garnett, would take over as the main influence on his writing. Jessie's service helped to make the third version of 'Paul Morel' into what became, after yet another rewriting following its rejection by Heinemann in July 1912, the published novel, *Sons and Lovers*. Not only did Lawrence write it, as she advised, 'with both hands earnestly', he even incorporated many of her recollections virtually word for word (Chambers, p. 198).[10] Her reactions on receiving the new version, 'a few sheets at a time', were at first enthusiastic. This would have been the early months of 1912, when Lawrence was living again in Eastwood, and when Ford's claimed visit would have taken place. Jessie writes:

> The early pages delighted me. Here was all that spontaneous flow, the seemingly effortless translation of life that filled me with admiration. His descriptions of family life were so vivid, so exact, and so concerned with everyday things we had never even noticed before. . . . It was his power to transmute the common experiences into significance that I always felt to be Lawrence's greatest gift. He did not distinguish between small and great happenings; the common round was full of mystery, awaiting interpretation. Born and bred of working people, he had the

rare gift of seeing them from within, and revealing them on their own plane. . . . I felt that Lawrence was coming into his true kingdom as a creative artist, and an interpreter of the people to whom he belonged. (Chambers, pp. 197–8)

Yet, as Jessie also suggests, the forces that were coming together in the writing of *Sons and Lovers*, and that had been evaded in the characters and situations of *The White Peacock* and even in the first versions of 'Paul Morel', while they were creating a novel of powerful originality were also becoming exposed as still living and still unresolved. Jessie as midwife to 'Paul Morel' intensified the problems that had existed prior to the death of Mrs Lawrence. 'I began to realize that whatever approach Lawrence made to me inevitably involved him in a sense of disloyalty to his mother. . . . It was a bond that definitely excluded me from the only position in which I could be of vital help to him.' (Chambers, p. 201) Having given Lawrence the key to the new novel, Jessie found herself treated in the writing not as part of the answer, as she would have hoped, but as part of the problem. 'The writing of it was fundamentally a terrific fight for a bursting of the tension. The break came in the treatment of Miriam. As the sheets of manuscript came rapidly to me I was bewildered and dismayed at that treatment.' (Chambers, p. 201)

Jessie, as Keith Sagar puts it, was for Lawrence at the beginning of 1912 'already part of his past'.[11] Ford had wanted Lawrence to write 'a course of workingman novels, the idea of which he found oppressive' (Nehls, p. 116). That, too, was part of the past. So was the long succession of other women and girls who had contributed to his literary development – Alice Dax, Louie Burrows, Helen Corke and many more. So was the living influence of his mother. He now had a novel in print and a second accepted for publication, and was also a published poet and short story writer. The writing of the third version of 'Paul Morel' and the meeting with Frieda marked the end of a long period of growth, and the beginning of another.

Here are two versions of the same incident, Walter Morel coming home after a day's drinking with his friend Jerry. The first is from the third draft of 'Paul Morel', written immediately after Jessie's adverse comments on the second draft. The other is from the manuscript of *Sons and Lovers*.

"Eleven! said Mrs Morel, aloud, and she braced herself up to bear the shrill striking of the clock-bell. The sewing was resumed. Three men sat on three front door steps, singing "Nearer my God to Thee" and "Dolly Daydream" as they faced the moon. In spite of herself, and though she had heard the drunken men serenade their own tipsiness with a hymn dozens of times, she sickened with weariness, with loathing of the fools. There was a quarrel somewhere – there was brawling. And from the top of the hill, from under the moon, the little sound of shouting as the "Three Tunns" turned out. And down the valley, towards the darkness, the nearer roistering from the "Palmerston Arms". And far-off shouts from the Mansfield high-road, as the men came out of 'Ellen's'. Mrs Morel listened to the shouting and chanting as the men descended the hillside straight upon her house. She looked up. It seemed they might burst in. The brass candlesticks shone wickedly. She resumed her sewing.

It is a question whether she was more intoxicated with suffering than her husband with drink. He came at about twenty past eleven. He was not drunk, but in that wound-up state of intoxication whose precise calm and equipoise is easily shaken, when a little readjustment is irritating to make, when real thwarting maddens. He was perfectly amiable and serene when he got to the garden gate. But the latch was hard to find, and then it was stiff, so he swore nastily. He was sufficiently drunk to be oblivious of everybody save himself.

There was a step up from the scullery to the kitchen. The kitchen door was open. He entered the scullery, a kind of porch, quite decently, but he stumbled up the step into the living room, into his wife's presence. He was not used to the house. She started up, a wave of madness going over her like flame.

"A nice way to come in! she cried.

"They shouldna put the fool's step there! he said loudly.

"It's not the step – it's the drunken nuisance that falls over it," she vibrated.

"Who's a drunken nuisance? he resented, bullying.

"Why, say you're not drunk! You haven't been boozing all day with that other drunken dirt, without."

"No, I haven't been boozing all day. It's where you make your mistake."

"Ph! It's very evident what you've been doing.'
"Oh is it – Oh! – Oh, is it! [12]

The next day was a work-day, and the thought of it put a damper on the men's spirits. Most of them, moreover, had spent their money. Some were already rolling dismally home, to sleep in preparation for the morrow. Mrs Morel, listening to their mournful singing, went indoors. Nine oclock passed, and ten, and still "the pair" had not returned. On a doorstep somewhere, a man was singing loudly, sliding up and down "Lead Kindly Light". Mrs Morel was always indignant with the drunken men, that they must sing that hymn when they got maudlin.

"As if 'Genevieve' weren't good enough," she said.

The kitchen was full of the scent of boiled herbs and hops. On the hob, a large black saucepan steamed slowly. Mrs Morel took a panchion, a great bowl of thick red earth, poured a heap of white sugar into the bottom, and then, straining herself to the weight, poured in the liquor.

Just then, Morel came in. He had been very jolly in the 'Nelson', but coming home had become irritable. He had not quite got over the miserable feeling of irritability and pain, after having slept on the ground when he was so hot; and this came on again now, in the open air. He did not know he was angry. But when the garden gate resisted his attempts to open it, he kicked it till he broke the latch. He entered just as Mrs Morel was pouring the infusion of herbs into the saucepan. Swaying slightly, he lurched against the table. The boiling liquor pitched. Mrs Morel started back.

"Good gracious," she cried, "coming home in his drunkenness!

"Comin' home in his what? he snarled, his hat over his eye.

Suddenly her blood rose in a jet.

"Say you're not drunk! she flashed.

She had put down the saucepan, and was stirring the sugar into the beer. He dropped his two hands heavily on the table, and thrust his face forward at her.

" 'Say you're not drunk' " he repeated. "Why nobody but a nasty little bitch like you 'ud 'ave such a thought."

"Well you've been boozing all day, so if you're not drunk by eleven oclock at night – " she replied, continuing to stir.

"I've not been boozing all day – I've not been boozing all day – it's where you make your mistake," he said, quietly, and nastily.

"It looks as if I made a mistake," she replied.

"Does it – does it – Oh – Oh indeed! – Oh! [13]

Already, in 'Paul Morel', Lawrence has made revisions. He originally wrote 'Lead Kindly Light', then replaced it, only to restore it in the last version. The candlesticks at first shone 'complacently', suggesting their indifference to Mrs Morel's state of mind, whereas 'wickedly' could ally them with the threat she fears from outside, but more likely is a preparation for the mood in which she receives her husband. Most significantly, though, Mrs Morel, hearing the hymn, 'bubbled with laughter, and then immediately burned in hate of the fools', as though Lawrence at first wished to portray a more complex response in her towards the men's drunkenness, but decided that to do so would diffuse the intensity of her feelings.

The strength of the first version compared, say, to much of *The White Peacock*, is in its firm placing within the consciousness of someone who is central to the scene and therefore to its impact on the reader, rather than peripheral to it, as Cyril is. First Mrs Morel, then Morel, are used as the emotional focus for the events described, until they meet and their respective feelings are released in dialogue. This structure to the scene is retained in the *Sons and Lovers* version. Each character, therefore, governs in turn the shaping of the language. With Mrs Morel, Lawrence is building up a state of tense expectation, from her bracing herself for the clock to the growing sounds from all parts of the town – singing, quarrelling, brawling, shouting, chanting. The tension is carried, too, in the relentless similarity of the sentences – 'And from the top of the hill', 'And down the valley', 'And far-off shouts from the Mansfield high-road'. They are not, in fact, strictly sentences, but rather a sequence of impressions that build up the threat to Mrs Morel as she sits alone. Then, at the end of the paragraph, as she looks up in fear of their bursting in, sees only the candlesticks, and resumes her sewing, the tension is not relieved, but rather held in the security of a domestic familiarity that nevertheless suggests more than itself with the carefully placed adverb 'wickedly'. The short sentences reinforce the fragility of the domestic reassurance, as if there is not sufficient ease to embark on a thought or impression of more than a few words.

And yet there are weaknesses. The description is not firmly enough placed within the constraints of Mrs Morel's feelings. The word 'roistering' has too detached a tone to it. It feels too self-consciously chosen, unlike the more everyday 'shouting and chanting'. And the naming of the pubs suggests not only a familiarity with places that should be anathema to her but distracts the reader's attention away from Mrs Morel, waiting and tense, to an intimacy with the scenes of the men's activities that is out of keeping with the emotional force of the paragraph and with the restrictedness of the room felt against the sounds from outside.

The paragraphs written from Morel's point of view are less sure. The first sentence reads very much like Cyril, particularly the opening words, 'It is a question whether', which are based on the feelings of neither character but on the narrative act itself, thus drawing attention to a self-conscious presence distancing and reducing the tension created through sympathy with Mrs Morel. This distance also inhibits sympathy with the father. One or two details begin to fix the scene from his point of view. The troublesome latch, after the ease of having 'got to the garden gate', slows down his progress, and the two stages of being 'hard to find' and then 'stiff' enact the difficulty of a drunken man trying to manage something requiring a little deftness. Even this is better handled in the second version, though, where the gate is less the cause of his anger than the factor that reveals to him the anger he already feels. 'He kicked it till he broke the latch' is a better manifestation of anger, too, than swearing nastily, and the published text's 'and broke the latch' better still, in that the kicking is no longer suggested as being intended to break the latch, and conveys the loosely perceived link between cause and effect that characterises drunkenness. Morel's stumbling on the step in the 'Paul Morel' version also gives the man's impression, but this is reduced by Lawrence's feeling it necessary to describe the scullery as 'a kind of porch' and by the sentence 'He was not used to the house' (an addition to the manuscript), which is unnecessary and generalises away from the particular intensity of the meeting which is just taking place. The language of the first Morel paragraph, too, is not felt through the character but rather imposed in the tones of a generalising narrator – 'that wound-up state of intoxication whose precious calm and equipoise is easily shaken . . . ' – where the diction is far beyond the range of the character being described.

Lawrence's inability, or unwillingness, to sympathise with Mr Morel in 'Paul Morel' is redeemed in *Sons and Lovers* through replacing the attempt to describe his 'state of intoxication' by the feelings of the man himself, simply stated, thus treating him more on a level with Mrs Morel. Her state of mind, moreover, has been created with more economy, more directness, and yet in a way that allows some of the sympathy of 'bubbled with laughter' back in a more controlled form. Gone are the names of the pubs and the sounds of drunkenness from all quarters of the town, and instead we have one man singing, 'sliding up and down' (replaced in the published text by 'in a drawl'), which removes the threat of the shouting and chanting, or of bursting into the room. We have already been given an insight into the men's drinking with the dampening thought of the 'work-day'. It is no longer closing time, as it was in 'Paul Morel', and the men are coming home early with 'the morrow' in mind. Drinking, in fact, has been put into a perspective that also includes sleep and work, and the high spirits of one are undercut by the knowledge of the other. The world of the men remains relentlessly separate from that of the women, but the solitary singer is now a poignant figure, and his choice of song, while it angers Mrs Morel, is one point at which their worlds could touch. His emptiness and loneliness match hers, and it is her own state of mind that resists their appeal.

Lawrence has reshaped these early paragraphs with some subtlety, then, to allow the reader to feel more than just injured resentment on Mrs Morel's behalf, for we have been given a way to sympathise first with the men in general, then with the singer and so with Morel himself, and to do so by a means that excludes Mrs Morel. We can recognise, in other words, that, as Ada suggested, the mother's intolerance carried some blame for the father's behaviour. A crucial change here is in Mrs Morel's activity as she waits. In 'Paul Morel' she is sewing, the picture of the passive woman to whom the active male will return with noise and aggression. She is the injured party in waiting. In *Sons and Lovers* she is herself active, and engaged in activity that requires effort and judgement in her own right: she pours the sugar (later it is 'streamed'), she strains herself to the weight of the pan. Her work puts her more on a level with the men, while the concentration on her effort is also the measure of the strength that will be exerted against Morel. She is in the kitchen now, surrounded by the objects of her work, and they too have a forceful presence: the 'large black saucepan' on the hob, the 'great bowl of thick red earth', and the steaming and scent to which she has given rise. This is her territory far more than the 'living room' with its candlesticks and its striking clock. The tension, too, is located not only in the emotion of the character but in the nature of her activity at the moment of the husband's entering, and Lawrence's paragraph describing Morel's coming home holds the crucial moment of the lifting of the pan until the dropping of the whole thing seems inevitable. After this, the gentle lurch against the table with the pitching of the liquor is both an unexpectedly slight release and at the same time sufficient provocation for the readiness of the woman against the intruder.

The conversation that follows in each version is the expression, finally, of the aggression felt on each side, but the second is remarkable not so much for any change in what is said but rather for its brevity and for the increasing amount of narrative description. Indeed, in the manuscript Lawrence has subsequently cut the last four speeches of the extract along with another ten that originally followed. (All of these cuts are confirmed by Garnett in his marginal marks.) Lawrence, having relied in 'Paul Morel' on dialogue to develop character and situation (and the conversation continues for another two pages of manuscript through to the end of the fragment, with only one paragraph of six lines of narration), manages in *Sons and Lovers* to prepare so well in advance of the meeting that dialogue can be used more sparingly, just building up the tension sufficiently for the crisis in the scene, one published page later, when Morel shuts his wife out of the house (p. 34). At the same time, we are seeing Lawrence moving towards the methods of his later fiction in which he prefers to develop relationships between characters through narrative description of thoughts, feelings and actions (as he does in the 'Anna Victrix' chapter of *The Rainbow*), interspersed with dialogue, rather than relying on dramatisation through dialogue alone.

When Lawrence left England with Frieda in May 1912 he left behind not only all those things and people that were 'part of his past'. He left behind his career as a school teacher. His intention was to support himself and Frieda by writing. The rewriting of 'Paul Morel' was continuing during these months, with expected publication by Heinemann. Its rejection, while it meant yet another rewriting, also led to the emergence of Lawrence's first work of real literary quality from the promise of the rejected manuscript. In July Garnett sent Lawrence a set of notes on 'Paul Morel' which were to guide his revisions for publication by Duckworth. Lawrence commented that they were 'awfully nice and detailed. What a Trojan of energy and conscientiousness you are!' (*Letters*, I, 427) After the next rewriting Garnett also went through the final manuscript deleting over seventy passages. Many of these were passages of dialogue, but, as Mark Schorer summarises, there were other kinds of deletion.

> Out would go unnecessary bits of expository prose, merely repetitious scenes that did nothing to deepen characterization already established, awkward and tonally inept authorial intrusions. . . . He would cut passages in which the characterization (especially of Mrs Morel) was so unattractive that Lawrence risked the loss of his readers' sympathy for her. He would cut passages of shaky psychology as in the episode . . . where Lawrence imputes to the infant-in-arms his own adolescent revulsion from his father. Out would go material that was simply irrelevant to the novel's central concerns, like a long passage about William. . . .

Schorer concludes:

> On the evidence of this manuscript alone, one must conclude that Edward Garnett was a brilliant editor. He was cutting for reasons of length, to be sure, but in those cuttings he was also considering matters of tone, texture, thematic unity, reader response, even plausibility. . . . Every deletion that Garnett made seems to me to have been to the novel's advantage.[14]

Lawrence himself wrote to Garnett on receiving the first copy of *Sons and Lovers* in May 1913: 'The copy of *Sons and Lovers* has just come – I am fearfully proud of it. I reckon it is quite a great book. I shall not write quite in that style any more. It's the end of my youthful period. Thanks a hundred times.' (*Letters*, I, 551) The novel was dedicated to Garnett.

Many influences went into the writing and rewriting of *Sons and Lovers*, some of them to do with Lawrence himself, some involving the active contribution of other people. Jessie Chambers and Edward Garnett were two of the most prominent. When it was at last finished, the achievement for Lawrence was not only a style of writing but an attitude towards the novel form that included clarity of purpose and clarity of the methods by which his purpose could be achieved. From now on, it becomes possible to talk about Lawrence having a conception of the novel.

3 Lawrence's Conception of the Novel

Mary has gone with some cinematograph-filming people from the Bristol to climb Etna and peer down the crater. If she'll hop after Empedocles I'll write her an elegy. . . . She's cut her hair. One day it thundered and lightened and was very Etnaish, and it got on her nerves all alone in the Studio, so she went and bobbed herself. Frieda says it suits her, but ever since, I can't bear the sights of her. It brings out all the pseudo-mannish street-arab aggressive selfish insolence, which affects me nowadays, as a male, like somebody throwing black pepper in my eyes. I plainly hate her. She began a novel on the strength of it: opened in studio, where lovely strange lady cuts her long black locks and is spied upon through one of the port-holes by a thrilled and enthralled young gentleman: 'nice young thing, quite young and *full* of enthusiasm, *full* of enthusiasm, and clean, hardly seen a woman before: that kind of thing' (Quot.) – You see which way the minds of these elderly hankering bitches turns. – But I set my foot on that nasty worm of a novel, and killed it. – Conceit, hideous, elderly, megalomaniac sexual conceit, that's what ails these elderly scavenging bitches. If Etna had any sense of fitness he'd spit a fat mouthful of lava at her. (*Letters*, III, 551–2)

Mary is Mary Cannan, and her novel, as Lawrence describes it, with its basis in self-regard, its idealised characters, and its blend of hygiene and voyeurism, is exactly the kind of poisonous creature on which he would wish to set his foot. Emotional dishonesty and sexual wish fulfilment are two human failings against which his own fiction is particularly directed, especially in the period after his elopement with Frieda. What is particularly effective in this letter is the way that Mary is developed through a mixture of revealing action (the bobbing of the hair, the parodic summary of her novel) and violent authorial interpretation, which is increasingly Lawrence's method of characterisation after *Sons and Lovers*. Mary, in her crippling vanity and in Lawrence's attitude towards her as typifying 'sexual conceit', is as striking a creation as Hermione Roddice, or Mrs Witt in *St Mawr*.

By June 1920, when Lawrence wrote these remarks in a letter from Sicily to his new friend Jan Juta, the painter, he had published, since *Sons and Lovers* in 1913, only one novel, *The Rainbow*, and that had been suppressed by court order in November 1915 a month and a half after publication. *Women in Love*, however, was at proof stage, he was just finishing *The Lost Girl*, and was about to begin writing *Aaron's Rod*. He had also worked, at various periods, on *The Insurrection of Miss Houghton* and *Mr Noon* as well as a large number of stories. *The Prussian Officer* collection had been published by Duckworth in November 1914. Novels still to come included *Kangaroo* (1923), *The Plumed Serpent* (1926) and *Lady Chatterley's Lover* (1928), and several collections of stories and novellas. During these fifteen years of his career, between 1913 and 1928, the year that saw the end of *Lady Chatterley* and of *The Man Who Died*, there is great variety in his work, both in subject and in style.

Lawrence developed as rapidly after his elopement with Frieda as during the years of rewriting 'Paul Morel', and new people and new ideas naturally had their influence on his writing. Most of his novels were rewritten and revised over a considerable period of time. *Women in Love* was begun as *The Sisters* early in 1913. His work on it, however, necessitated the writing of *The Rainbow* to provide a past life for Ursula Brangwen. This was finished by March 1915. He returned to *The Sisters* a year later in very different mood and circumstances, disillusioned by the war, by events and attitudes in England, by his own poverty and dependence on friends for a home, and not least by the reception given to *The Rainbow*. What was intended in 1913 to be 'a new, lighter novel' (*Letters*, I, 530), and 'rather more cheerful than *Sons and Lovers*' *Letters*, I, 538), had become something very different, what Keith Sagar calls 'a misanthropic, apocalyptic novel'.[1] Frieda wanted this version to be called *Dies Irae*, the day of wrath (*Letters*, II,

669). Successive revisions developed and then modified even this. The novel was also, at first, like *The White Peacock*, written in the first person (*Letters*, I, 550). *The Rainbow*, too, changed in both conception and treatment over the much shorter period of its writing. Lawrence did not at first realise how large a task he had undertaken, and for a long while thought in terms of only one novel. Only as late as January 1915 did he decide to 'split the book into two volumes' (*Letters*, II, 256), which meant that the work would end not with Ursula's marriage but with her vision of the rainbow. Lawrence was apparently not happy with his handling of this vision, reworking it even during the proof stage. As John Worthen puts it:

> The last pages are trying both to end a novel deprived of its original end, and to be a triumphant public utterance. Lawrence modified them a good deal in revision; when he finished the last paragraph in March, Ursula 'knew . . . that the new growth should take place, the vast forest of mankind should spring up urgent and young out of the brittle, marshy foulness of the old corruption'; the ending we now know must have been introduced at the proof stage, in August.[2]

The published ending, however, was itself changed in Lawrence's own hand in the copy of the book he gave to his sister Ada. Ursula now 'knew that the fight was to the good. It was not to annihilation but at last to newness. She knew in the rainbow that the fight was to the good.' (Delavenay, p. 381)

To speak of Lawrence's conception of the novel, then, is made difficult both by the variety of writing that he produced during the major phase of his career and by his changes in intention as he wrote and rewrote his drafts. Even when we focus on a single work, we usually find apparently incompatible modes of writing alongside each other, as the narrative of *St Mawr* is disturbed by Lou Witt's vision of evil, and by the long history of the ranch, Las Chivas. At the same time Lawrence did maintain a strong and consistent attitude towards the purpose of writing, and some consideration of this serves to clarify not only what he was trying to achieve in his work but also the reasons for the tensions that often exist within a Lawrence text.

Most of Lawrence's essays and articles on novel-writing date from one year, 1925, and even from the same month, June, when he had finished correcting the page proofs of *St Mawr* and had written the play *David*. During the next month he was to write most of the essays in *Reflections on the Death of a Porcupine*. The significant essays for the novel of June 1925 are 'Art and Morality', 'Morality and the Novel', 'Why the Novel Matters', 'The Novel and the Feelings' and 'The Novel', which was later included in *Reflections on the Death of a Porcupine*.[3] Of his major novels, only *Lady Chatterley's Lover* remained to be written. Yet this is not an instance of the writer turning critic after his creativity has been expended, for in an important respect Lawrence's writing had always been critical, not only in letters and occasional writing, but in the fiction itself. As he puts it in the foreword to *Fantasia of the Unconscious*, 'The novels and poems come unwatched out of one's pen. And then the absolute need which one has for some sort of satisfactory mental attitude towards oneself and things in general makes one try to abstract some definite conclusions from one's experience as a writer and as a man.' (p. 15) What we find in the essays of 1925 is a characteristically vigorous set of polemics that makes explicit his practice and attitudes over the previous fifteen or so years.

One of Lawrence's earliest public statements on the purpose of art is the paper 'Art and the Individual', read at a meeting in Eastwood in 1908.[4] Towards the end of the short piece he asks the question 'What then is the mission of art?' This is his answer, and it is one that remains as a governing principle over the span of his writing life.

> To bring us into sympathy with as many men, as many objects, as many phenomena as possible. To be in sympathy with things is to some extent to acquiesce in their purpose, to help on that purpose. We want, we are for ever trying to unite ourselves with the whole universe, to carry out some ultimate purpose – evolution, we call one phase of the carrying out. The passion of human beings to be brought into sympathetic understanding of one another is stupendous; witness it in the eagerness with which biographies, novels, personal and subjective writings are read. Emotion tends to issue in action. (*Phoenix II*, 226)

The very phrasing of the question is characteristic of the writer whose mission was to be to make 'folk – English folk

– . . . alter, and have more sense' (*Letters*, I, 544). The answer picks up several key features of his preoccupations as a didactic writer: sympathy, ultimate purpose, human passion, and the novel as one major form in which the exploration of human subjectivity is to be conducted.

The demand for sympathy is prominent in 'Morality and the Novel':

> The business of art is to reveal the relation between man and his circumambient universe, at the living moment. . . . If we think about it, we find that our life *consists in* this achieving of a pure relationship between ourselves and the living universe about us. This is how I save my soul" by accomplishing a pure relationship between me and another person, me and other people, me and a nation, me and a race of men, me and the animals, me and the trees or flowers, me and the earth, me and the skies and sun and stars, me and the moon. . . . This, if we knew it, is our life and our eternity: the subtle, perfected relation between me and my whole circumambient universe. (*Phoenix*, pp. 527–8)

And yet sympathy, for Lawrence, can also apparently include emotions like hatred. To feel hatred, just as much as to feel love, is to 'acquiesce' in the purpose of men, objects and phenomena.

> *All* emotions go to the achieving of a living relationship between a human being and the other human being or creature or thing he becomes purely related to. All emotions, including love and hate, and rage and tenderness, go to the adjusting of the oscillating, unestablished balance between two people who amount to anything. (*Phoenix*, p. 529)

So, of the novels of Thomas Hardy, Lawrence writes that all of his heroes and heroines 'are struggling hard to come into being', and that 'the first and chiefest factor is the struggle into love and the struggle with love: by love, meaning the love of a man for a woman and a woman for a man' (*Phoenix*, p. 410). To experience any degree of sympathy, in Lawrence's view, of love or hatred, is to enter into a real relationship with the 'circumambient universe' and to help 'into being' not only oneself but the other with whom the sympathy is felt.

The emphasis on 'living' – 'the living moment', 'a living relationship' – is, for Lawrence, one that is inescapably made by the novel, 'the highest example of subtle inter-relatedness that man has discovered' (*Phoenix*, p. 528). This is because in a novel, as he argues in 'Why the Novel Matters', 'the characters can do nothing but *live*. If they keep on being good, according to pattern, or bad, according to pattern, or even volatile, according to pattern, they cease to live, and the novel falls dead. A character in a novel has got to live, or it is nothing.' (*Phoenix*, p. 537) We should, then, 'Turn truly, honourably to the novel, and see wherein you are man alive, and wherein you are dead man in life' (*Phoenix*, p. 537), because the novel is a true test of the difference between life and 'just existence' (*Phoenix*, p. 529).

> To be alive, to be man alive, to be whole man alive: that is the point. And at its best, the novel, and the novel supremely, can help you. It can help you not to be a dead man in life. So much of a man walks about dead and a carcass in the street and house, today. . . . But in the novel you can see, plainly, when the man goes dead, the woman goes inert. You can develop an instinct for life, if you will, instead of a theory of right and wrong, good and bad. (*Phoenix*, pp. 537–8)

When Lawrence looked at the England of his day, during the periods he lived there, he too often saw a people going dead. This was something he felt particularly strongly during the First World War. He writes in 1915 from Ripley in Derbyshire to Lady Ottoline Morrell of the working men of the region.

> Altogether the life here is so dark and violent: it all happens in the senses, powerful and rather destructive: no mind nor mental consciousness, unintellectual. These men are passionate enough, sensuous, dark – God, how all my boyhood comes back – so violent, so dark, the mind always dark and without understanding, the senses violently active. It makes me sad beyond words. These men, whom I love so much – and the life has such a power over me – they *understand* mentally so horribly: only industrialism, only wages and

money and machinery. They can't *think* anything else. (*Letters*, II, 489)

This was three months after the suppression of *The Rainbow*. Shortly before that happened, he had written to Lady Ottoline in terms that recall the end of that novel, with Ursula's vision of 'new germination' (p. 495).

It is the new year one wants so badly; let the old die altogether, completely. It is only the new spring I care about, opening the hard little buds that seem like stone, in the souls of people. They must open and a new world begin. But first there is the shedding of the old, which is so slow and so difficult, like a sickness. I Ind it so difficult to let the old life go, and to wait for the new life to take form. But it begins to take form now. It is not any more such a fierce question of shedding away. (*Letters*, II, 388)

He had even felt, back in December 1914, that the war could be of benefit in making people turn to the kind of literature that would help them to 'let the old life go'.

I am glad of this war. It kicks the pasteboard bottom in the usual 'good' popular novel. People have felt much more deeply and strongly these last few months, and they are not going to let themselves be taken in by 'serious' works whose feeling is shallower than that of the official army reports. . . . Folk will either read sheer rubbish, or something that has in it as much or more emotional force as the newspaper has in *it* today. I am glad of the war. It sets a slump in trifling. If Lucas reads my novel, he ought to *know* how good it is. And he ought to respect it. (*Letters*, II, 240)

Lucas was reader for the publisher Methuen, and the novel, which he accepted, was *The Rainbow*.

The factors, then, that are important in Lawrence's conception of the novel are 'emotional force', meaning those features of the content that concern the living feelings of the characters, and the intention to bring about a 'new spring' in the minds and souls of his countrymen. As he writes to Garnett in February 1913, 'I think, do you know, I have inside me a sort of answer to the *want* of today: to the real, deep want of the English people, not to just what they fancy they want. And gradually, I shall get my hold on them.' (*Letters*, I, 511) For that new spring to 'take form', the novel itself must adapt in order to present real emotions with the force necessary to make readers see their own 'deep want'. In 'Surgery for the Novel – or a Bomb', Lawrence concludes:

> The novel has a future. It's got to have the courage to tackle new propositions without using abstractions; it's got to present us with new, really new feelings, a whole line of new emotion, which will get us out of the emotional rut. Instead of snivelling about what is and has been, or inventing new sensations in the old line, it's got to break a way through, like a hole in the wall. (*Phoenix*, p. 520)

But if the novel must be a dynamic force, it must also be a balanced one if it is to remain an honest, or moral, work. There will be tension between the life of the characters, for example, and the intention of the writer to make them mean, or between the emotions treated and the feelings of the novelist on behalf of one particular emotion, with the danger of his failing to recognise that all real emotions are equally valid. This is what Lawrence has in mind when he speaks of the novelist putting 'his thumb in the scale, to pull down the balance to his own predilection' (*Phoenix*, p. 528). The beauty of the novel is that 'everything is true in its own relationship, and no further', and yet 'the relatedness and inter-relatedness of all things flows and changes and trembles like a stream' (*Phoenix II*, 422). This, for Lawrence, makes the novel 'the highest example of subtle inter-relatedness that man has discovered'. In the novel 'Everything is true in its own time, place, circumstance, and untrue outside of its own place, time, circumstance. If you try to nail anything down, in the novel, either it kills the novel, or the novel gets up and walks away with the nail.' And morality, he continues, 'is the trembling instability of the balance' (*Phoenix*, p. 528). So he is able to conclude his essay on 'Morality and the Novel' with the memorable assertion that 'The novel is the perfect medium for revealing to us the changing rainbow of our living relationships. The novel can help us to live as nothing else can. . . . ' (*Phoenix*, p. 532)

Keith Sagar, writing about the genesis of *The Rainbow*, speaks of Lawrence's theory that

> Since . . . all the great conflicting opposites which motivate human beings are equally valid, all the beliefs and life-modes embodied in the novel have their countervailing opposites. It is a 'dynamic idea' which naturally translates into the dynamics of a novel, a novel's pattern of stresses and balances, gains and losses, within individuals, between individuals, between generations, between individuals and their society, between man and God.[5]

Here is one version of that sense of dislocation discussed in Chapter 1 in relation to the modern literary consciousness, but made essential to the conception and execution of the novel as a work of art. The 'stresses and balances' within Lawrence's 'perfect medium' exist and are played out in terms of the lives of the characters and in respect of the novelist's attitude towards them, while at the same time a second dimension of stress will derive from his attitude towards his readers.

What is fundamental to the execution of any novel is the writer's handling of language. Language, before any other feature of the finished work, is the medium through which 'stresses and balances' operate to enact the 'dynamics' of the novel, and if Lawrence expressed strong opinions about what the novel should be doing, he also had clear, if changing, ideas about the proper use of literary language.

John Worthen says that Lawrence needs 'a special language' to write about the experiences with which *The Rainbow* is concerned, 'and accordingly he invents it'.[6] Lawrence quite explicitly saw himself as 'inventing' language, both in terms of the functions he expected language to perform from novel to novel, and in the ways he adapted and refined – reinvented – language and linguistic forms as he rewrote each novel over months and years. Looking back, for example, at the end of 1913 on the style of *Sons and Lovers*, he described it as 'that hard, violent style full of sensation and presentation', while 'The Wedding Ring' was to be '*very* different', and 'written in another language almost' (*Letters*, II, 132). This was subsequently referred to as 'the exhaustive method', and was contrasted with the alternative of writing 'pure object and story' (*Letters*, II, 143). In the same letter, written to Edward Garnett from Italy in January 1914, Lawrence has a further comment on his method of writing in *Sons and Lovers*, which expands on what he means by 'full of sensation and presentation'. 'I have', he says, 'no longer the joy in creating vivid scenes, that I had in *Sons and Lovers*. I don't care much more about accumulating objects in the powerful light of emotion, and making a scene of them. I have to write differently.' (*Letters*, II, 142). As late as 1925, in the essay 'The Novel and the Feelings', Lawrence complains that we 'have no language for the feelings', that 'our feelings do not even exist for us' (*Phoenix*, p. 757). In the contrast between 'making a scene' of objects in the light of emotion and 'the exhaustive method' we have not only a change from Mrs Morel's candlesticks or saucepan and the emotional function they serve in the scene of Walter Morel's drunken return home. We have a stage in the constant debate and experiment in Lawrence's writing about ways of portraying feelings.

A short example from *The Rainbow* clarifies the kind of writing Lawrence means by 'the exhaustive method'. I choose not one of the denser passages from 'Anna Victrix', but a paragraph from the first of the two chapters called 'The Widening Circle', here dealing with the girlhood of Ursula. Will Brangwen in a moment of anger has hit his daughter across her face with a duster.

> Her heart burnt in isolation, like a watchfire lighted. She did not forget, she did not forget, she never forgot. When she returned to her love for her father, the seed of mistrust and defiance burned unquenched, though covered up far from sight. She no longer belonged to him unquestioned. Slowly, slowly, the fire of mistrust and defiance burned in her, burned away her connexion with him. (p. 267)

Here in a miniature form is an example of the kind of repetition Lawrence defends in his 1919 'Foreword to *Women in Love*'.

> In point of style, fault is often found with the continual, slightly modified repetition. The only answer is that it is natural to the author: and that every natural crisis in emotion or passion or understanding comes from this pulsing, frictional to-and-fro, which works up to culmination. (*Phoenix II*, 276)

The crisis developed in *The Rainbow* passage concerns not only emotional pain but an awareness within Ursula of difference between herself and her father. The awareness is itself a beginning of a kind of self-consciousness in her, for she is both separate and determined to remain so: the three main clauses of 'She did not forget, she did not forget, she never forgot' reflect her resoluteness. Equally her resolution to be resolute is itself a part of the change that is assimilated by the third modified repetition with its unexpectedly altered verb form. A child determining not to forget is suddenly and momentarily seen from a far distant perspective: 'she never forgot'. At the same time her self-consciousness is suggested in the image of the watchfire, which at once captures both the pain and the watchfulness that smoulder in her. This image, as so often in Lawrence, reaches out to incorporate other images: 'the seed of mistrust' also burns, though that is not what seeds normally do. What these repetitions and merging images are building towards is the only straightforward statement of the passage: 'She no longer belonged to him unquestioned.' This, in fact, is what the paragraph is saying, yet the mere statement is not an adequate way of saying it. The working round, both describing and suggesting emotional complexity, is as important a part of what has happened as the brief statement that actually clarifies it. Even then the statement is not the end of the matter, but has to be moved away from with the last sentence of the paragraph that returns to the fire image in a pattern of repeating words and rhythms. And we realise that 'The Widening Circle', with *its* image of ripples moving away from a centre of impact, has been created in the development of this particular feature of emotional change within the writing of the paragraph. Lawrence is portraying feelings at moments of crisis, and the repercussions of events, relatively insignificant in themselves, are what give 'the exhaustive method' its material and make 'The Widening Circle' so apt a title for two of the chapters of this novel. In contrast, the titles of the chapters dealing with corresponding stages of Paul Morel's development, 'The Young Life of Paul' and 'Paul Launches Into Life', are descriptive in a much narrower way, without the suggestiveness of a consciously adopted stylistic method.

Lawrence was aware that the change from 'presentation' in his writing left him open to the charge of vagueness. In his letter to

Garnett of January 1914 he expands on the idea.

> I write with everything vague – plenty of fire underneath,
> but, like bulbs in the ground, only shadowy flowers that must
> be beaten and sustained, for another spring. – I feel that this
> second half of the Sisters is very beautiful, but it may not
> be sufficiently incorporated to please you. I do not try to
> incorporate it very much – I prefer the permeating beauty.
> It is my transition stage – but I must write to live, and it
> must produce its flowers, and if they be frail or shadowy,
> they will be all right if they are true to their hour. (*Letters*,
> II, 143)

Yet the final impression of *The Rainbow* is not one of
vagueness, nor is it of 'frail or shadowy' flowers. Lawrence, at
this stage, is writing defensively, and in doing so understates the
'dynamic idea' behind his method. In the 'Foreword to *Women
in Love*', with *The Rainbow* written, published and banned, he
is unashamedly forthright on the significance of his art.

> Man struggles with his unborn needs and fulfilment. New
> unfoldings struggle up in torment in him, as buds struggle forth
> from the midst of a plant. Any man of real individuality tries to
> know and to understand what is happening, even in himself,
> as he goes along. This struggle for verbal consciousness should
> not be left out in art. It is a very great part of life. It is not
> superimposition of a theory. It is the passionate struggle into
> conscious being. (*Phoenix II*, 276)

The strength of Lawrence's use of language in the novel is in the
daring with which he attempts to embody emotional changes so
that the 'struggle into conscious being' is properly understood in all
its tortuousness. If part of the process involves the writer coming to
terms with 'what is happening, even in himself', then that is one
guarantee of his flowers being 'true to their hour'. Writing is *his*
'struggle for verbal consciousness' as much as it is the enactment
of consciousness in his characters and its forceful communication
to his readers. It is all part of helping on the purpose of 'as many
men, as many objects, as many phenomena as possible'. The 'pure

elationship' to be achieved between 'me and another person, me
and other people, me and a nation' depends, ultimately, upon the
development of a relationship between the writer and his writing,
between the user of language and the structure and texture of the
language used.

4 The Language of Prose

Against the background of Lawrence's conception of the novel, we can now go on to look at some of the characteristic features of language as it is used in his fiction, both in the novels and in the short stories. Naturally, it will not be possible to cover anything but the briefest of selections from the enormous range of his writing. I have tried to select those features and those examples that are typical of the kinds of uses to which he puts language, and to explain how it is that English can be adapted as Lawrence adapts it, and why he chooses to do so in specific instances. I shall be discussing first of all some of the ways words can be combined into groups in the writing of sentences, and then something of the relationships that are possible between different parts of sentences.[1]

The two main groupings of words in English sentences are nominal groups and verbal groups. At the simplest level, the verbal groups convey information about what has happened, including, through tense, when it happened, while the nominal groups deal with who or what were in some way associated with its happening, and are those phrases or individual words that could stand as the subject of a clause. This holds for all three sentence types, statements (otherwise known as declarative sentences), questions (interrogative) and commands (imperative), though imperative sentences in particular frequently depend for their sense upon recognition of omitted items of grammar, such as 'you'. (Many writers, however, Lawrence included, write at times in incomplete sentences in order to achieve a particular effect, in which case we have to account for the effect in terms of the disruption of our normal expectation of sentences.)

In modern English, the nominal groups are capable of a great deal of expansion. The only essential item of the group is the headword (the noun in traditional grammar), but this will often be accompanied by a determiner ('the', 'an', 'that', 'her') and one or more modifiers and/or qualifiers. Modifiers, which are almost always single words, precede the headword, while qualifiers are usually phrases and follow it. At the beginning of *The Rainbow*, the group 'the heated, blind intercourse of farm-life' (p. 8) consists of a headword, 'intercourse', a determiner, 'the', two separate modifiers, 'heated' and 'blind', and a qualifier, 'of farm-life'. It could, in theory , have any number of modifiers and qualifiers, and it is this capacity which enables the nominal group to carry the weight of descriptive information in English writing.

Here, for example, is a passage from 'The Captain's Doll', which Lawrence was writing towards the end of 1921. Captain Hepburn's room is described in his absence through the experience of Hannele and Mitchka.

> The room was really beautiful, spacious, pale, soft-lighted. It was heated by a large stove of dark-blue tiles, and had very little furniture save large peasant cupboards or presses of painted wood, and a huge writing-table, on which were writing materials and some scientific apparatus and a cactus plant with fine scarlet blossoms. But it was a man's room. Tobacco and pipes were on a little tray, on the pegs in the distance hung military overcoats and belts, and two guns on a bracket. Then there were two telescopes, one mounted on a stand near a window. Various astronomical apparatus lay upon the table. (*Three Novellas*, p. 163)

The first nominal group, 'the room', simply consists of a determiner and a headword, but after this almost all the important information, everything that gives the reader the look and feel of the room, is conveyed through nominal groups of varying construction. In 'a large stove of dark-blue tiles' we have determiner, modifier, headword and the qualifier 'of dark-blue tiles', which itself consists of a subordinate nominal group where 'dark-blue' acts as a modifier to the headword 'tiles'. The same pattern is present in 'large peasant cupboards or presses of painted wood', except that the two modifiers, 'large' and 'peasant', and the qualifier, 'of painted wood', are made to apply to what are in effect alternative headwords, 'cupboards or presses'. It is as if Lawrence is offering the reader a choice of what they should be called, perhaps reflecting some uncertainty in the writing of a description that is supposedly seen through the eyes of native German speakers. There are other patterns, too, of the nominal group. In 'very little furniture' there is no determiner and no qualifier, but instead a modifier, 'little', with an intensifier, 'very'. The phrase, of course, is more colloquial than most of its context, for we understand by Lawrence's words not that the room contained very small furniture, which is the more literal meaning, but that there was not much of it! There is also the series of three nominal groups all acting as complements to 'were': 'writing materials' (modifier, headword), 'some scientific apparatus' (determiner, modifier, headword), 'a cactus plant with fine scarlet blossoms' (determiner, modifier, headword, qualifier consisting of preposition, modifier, modifier, headword). A comparison of the variety and frequency of the nominal groups with the verb forms in the paragraph will confirm the major contribution of these phrases in straightforward descriptive writing such as this. Almost all the main verbs are forms of the verb 'to be', and in two cases 'were' and 'was' are auxiliaries to the main verbs 'heated' in the second sentence and 'mounted' in the penultimate. The exceptions are 'had', 'hung' and 'lay'. The verbs, in fact, are largely functional, providing the basic grammatical structure for the sentences but not conveying information or mood in their own right. The impact of the writing, its visual effects, its balance, even its changes in rhythm, are due to Lawrence's handling of nominal groups.

Unlike nominal groups, verbal groups are not capable of a great deal of expansion. The possible constituents of a verbal group are the auxiliary, such as 'had', 'should', 'might', the verb, which is the only essential element, and the extension, such as 'on', 'up', 'away'. In 'The gipsy man had been sitting loosely on the side of his cart', the verbal group 'had been sitting' consists of two auxiliaries, 'had' and 'been', and the verb 'sitting', while 'He now jumped softly down from the shaft' consists of the verb, 'jumped', and the extension 'down' (*The Virgin and the Gipsy* in *St Mawr and the Virgin and the Gipsy*, p. 185). Two auxiliaries are usually the maximum in Modern English, though in theory several more ('might have been being') are possible. Similarly, it is hard to think of more than one extension in normal usage.

There is, therefore, some capacity for variety in the construction of verbal groups, but not the opportunity for suggestive expansion that characterises the nominal group.

What the verbal group can do, however, is to increase or diminish the tension of a passage by the frequency and variety of verb forms, by delay and omission, and by surprise. Naturally, the exploitation of the possibilities of the verbal group is more often found in writing about action or mental behaviour than in description, where low-key effects are usually more appropriate. Equally, through its control of tense, the verbal group has the scope to provide variety over time, giving depth to a simple narrative. A straightforward example is from *St Mawr*: 'Lou escaped to look at St Mawr. He was still moist where the saddle had been. And he seemed a little bit extinguished, as if virtue had gone out of him' (*St Mawr and The Virgin and the Gipsy*, p. 60). Here the simple past of the main narrative ('escaped', 'was' and 'seemed') is expressed with neither auxiliaries nor extensions. Depth, in terms of a more distant past that is encroaching upon Lou's observations and consciousness, is provided in the pluperfect verb forms, 'had been', which consists of auxiliary and verb, and 'had gone out', which has auxiliary, verb and extension. We also have the infinitive form 'to look at', allowing intention to be shown behind Lou's actions. Memory, observation and motivation are all essential to the convincing portrayal of character and the writer's skill in suggesting these factors at work depends to a large extent on this subtle handling of verb forms.

It is noticeable in the above passage how little reliance there is on nominal groups for the effect of the writing. Variety is provided in the play with verb forms, but the tone is still low-key. If we now look at a passage of considerable tension and excitement, we shall see how daring manipulation of both verbal and nominal groups can produce a high level of involvement for the reader. In *Women in Love*, Hermione, driven by frustration over the gradual breakdown of her relationship with Birkin, is brought to the point of physically assaulting him with a paper-weight.

Then swiftly, in a flame that drenched down her body like fluid lightning and gave her a perfect, unutterable consummation, unutterable satisfaction, she brought down the ball of jewel stone with all her force, crash on his head. But her fingers were in the way and deadened the blow. Nevertheless down went his head on the table on which his book lay, the stone slid aside and over his ear, it was one convulsion of pure bliss for her, lit up by the crushed pain of her fingers. But it was not somehow complete. She lifted her arm high to aim once more, straight down on the head that lay dazed on the table. She must smash it, it must be smashed before her ecstasy was consummated, fulfilled for ever. A thousand lives, a thousand deaths mattered nothing now, only the fulfilment of this perfect ecstasy. (*Women in Love*, pp. 117–18)

Three features demand particular attention here: the vocabulary, the variety achieved through the handling of nominal and verbal groups, and the prose rhythms such variety produces. There is, for example, a degree of fluidity between verb and nominal forms: 'consummation' first appears as headword of the group 'unutterable consummation', with a modifier that is itself formed from a verb, and then reappears as the verb in the group 'was consummated'; similarly 'fulfilled' is a verb followed by the adverbial group 'for ever', and in the next sentence is the headword 'fulfilment'. Some of the verbs make surprising choices: the flame 'drenched', her bliss is 'lit up' by the pain of her fingers. We also find unusual combinations of modifiers with headwords and qualifiers: 'Luid lightning'; 'one convulsion of pure bliss', where the headword 'convulsion' is in some tension with the qualifier 'of pure bliss'; 'crushed pain', where the modifier is a form of the verb and thus suggests the way the pain was caused as much as the pain itself. These surprises keep the reader in a state of alertness, and by disturbing the verbal texture of the writing help in the enactment of Hermione's own state of heightened excitement.

The nominal and verbal groups in the passage display considerable variety in their use and form. The first sentence is remarkable in making the reader wait for so long before coming to the main verb 'brought down'. Lawrence, having told us that the action is performed 'swiftly', deals first with the flame that 'drenched down' (verb, extension) and 'gave' (verb) such satisfaction, as if it is perhaps the enjoyment of the flame that is the most intense part of the experience. The lingering over 'a perfect, unutterable consummation, unutterable satisfaction' would support this, though when the main verb does come its impact is all the more forceful for the contrived delay, and its reverberations are drawn out over the rest of the sentence. Of the nominal groups that follow, 'the ball of jewel stone' is particularly interesting in that the headword, 'ball', is less striking than the phrase 'jewel stone' in the subordinate nominal group that acts as qualifier to 'ball'. We are invited to visualise not the plain 'ball' but the visually suggestive 'jewel stone', and while the headword 'ball' does alliterate with the verb 'brought' which it complements, its strength is outweighed by the three syllables of 'jewel stone'. Lawrence has thrown the balance of the whole group awry, which again poses a question concerning the true focus of Hermione's satisfaction. The actual hitting of Birkin, which is supposed to be the release of her frustrations, is apparently less important than the peripheral details of the deed: her feelings as she prepares, the object used, the practicalities of how not to do it! Her feeling is intense and takes her, for once in the novel, out of herself, out of her own head, but practical realities endanger and diffuse the emotional intensity. Just as her fingers get 'in the way' of the blow, so the adverbial phrase that describes her bringing the ball down 'with all her force' loses *its* force by being separated from its verb by the nominal group 'the ball of jewel stone'.

Two other sentences deserve attention. The long third sentence, after the conjunction 'Nevertheless', consists of three main clauses each of which could be an independent sentence. The change of focus between the stone sliding aside and the 'convulsion of pure bliss' in fact risks making the sentence fall apart, especially as the final clause is subordinate to the 'convulsion'. The effect, however, is to convey something of Hermione's state of mind. She is scarcely capable of connected thought, and is merely receiving not quite connected impressions: the movement of the head, the book on the table, the movement of the stone, her own elation, and the pain. In keeping with this we have further disruption in the language: the inversion in the verbal group in the first clause, with the extension preceding the verb in 'down went his head', the dizzy alliteration of 'stone slid aside', and the unusual and clipped verbal group 'lit up', which looks back to the emotion at the beginning of the paragraph, the 'Lame' and the 'lightning'. The penultimate sentence, in which Hermione gathers herself for a second attempt, is remarkable for its use of verb forms. Apart from the headword 'ecstasy', all the impact in this sentence derives from the verbal groups with their repetitions and variations. 'She must smash it' consists of auxiliary and verb, but in a form in which the modal verb 'must' expresses determination. This is immediately followed by the same meaning expressed in the passive voice, 'it must be smashed', as if agency has somehow left Hermione herself and become a universal wish that this should be done. Then, at the end of the sentence, there is the very characteristic Lawrence device of making one auxiliary, 'was', serve two separate verbs, 'consummated' and 'fulfilled' – separate, but similar in meaning, so that Hermione's desire is lingered over as the different verbs 'work up to culmination' (*Phoenix II*, 276).

The working out of Lawrence's prose rhythms depends both upon the alternation of long and short sentences, and the variety of clauses and phrases achieved within sentences. In the above passage, for example, the long first sentence sets up a tension between waiting for the main verb that will satisfy the sense towards which the whole is moving, and the release already apparent in the long series of subordinate clauses that precedes the main clause. Repetition within the sentence, especially of a word like 'unutterable', slows the pace and reduces the urgency. When the movement is completed, moreover, the short flat second sentence, with its preponderance of monosyllabic words, threatens to render the effort already expended void. The rhythms of the third and fourth sentences are similarly played off against each other. The heaviness of 'Nevertheless' almost drags our attention to the consequences of the released energy, while the combination of a strong first consonant and long vowel sound in 'down' suggests a triumphant assertion of the achievement. At the same time, the occurrence of the extension ('down') before the verb ('went') or the subject ('his head') is disturbing, as if the movement is preceding that which is making the movement. This disturbance is reflected in the rhythm of the following phrases which are tacked together with a repeated preposition, 'on the table on which his book lay', where the lack of any kind of ease or smoothness in the grammar or diction gives a disconcerting sense of the state of shock under which Hermione is experiencing the events and making the observations. The short fourth sentence, beginning, like the second, with 'But', is blunt and rhythmically ungainly. Four monosyllabic words, alliterating on 't', are followed by two of two syllables, and the word 'somehow', in both sense and sound, inhibits any crispness of expression. The rhythmic sliding through not quite connected impressions in the third sentence has gathered into something firmer here, a realisation that disconnection has been present, yet the expression of incompleteness is itself, appropriately, incomplete. The rhythm of 'But it was not somehow complete' demands resolution, just as the action does, and both are provided in the movement that begins with the fifth sentence. Interestingly, though, the rhythms that begin to give assured fulfilment, with the nominal group 'her arm' and the adverb 'high' sustaining the momentum of the verb 'lifted', and the release enacted by the adverbial phrase 'straight down', are assurances of intention rather than of achievement. She does lift her arm, but she only intends to bring it down. The rhythms work, but the arm does not. A fulfilment of a kind is provided, for Hermione is able to recapture the emotion of the opening sentence and the reader is able to feel the resolution of the 'frictional to-and-fro' (*Phoenix II*, 276) of the rhythms. But nothing happens. Or rather Birkin has time to recover and shield himself from the second blow with a hastily snatched volume of Thucydides!

The effect of Lawrence's prose rhythms is not always, as it is here, to enable the reader to enter more fully into the experiences of one or more characters, but mood or emotion, even in a passage of plain description, is usually sustained in some way by the rhythmic variety of the writing. And variety is frequently a matter of the playing off of nominal and verbal groups within sentences, of maintaining a fluidity between nouns, verbs and adjectives, and of the careful balancing of long and short sentences.

One particular feature of English that is responsible to a large degree for allowing the sort of writing that Lawrence practises is subordination. The relation between clauses in Modern English, and between phrases and even between individual words, can be of co-ordination or of subordination. In Lawrence's work, there is also a tendency to make these the dominant relations between sentences – hence the 'fault often found with the continual, *slightly* modified repetition' (*Phoenix II*, 276). The elements in a co-ordinate structure are of equal status, and in fact either could stand alone and fulfil the same structural function within the sentence. A good example of co-ordination is in the following sentence from *The Plumed Serpent*:

The young Mexican who was accompanying the party was a professor in the University too: a rather short, soft young fellow of twenty-seven or eight, who wrote the inevitable poetry of sentiment, had been in the Government, even as a member of the House of Deputies, and was longing to go to New York. (p. 59)

There is co-ordination between the three clauses 'who wrote the inevitable poetry of sentiment', 'had been in the Government' and 'and was longing to go to New York'. Each stands in the same relation to the headword 'fellow'. Or, from the same novel, General Viedma is described: 'An odd, detached, yet cocky little man, a true little Indian, speaking Oxford English in a rapid, low, musical voice, with extraordinarily gentle intonation.' (p. 35) The sentence has no main verb, and is therefore not strictly speaking a sentence. This is itself not an unusual feature of Lawrence's writing. We also see the expansion of the nominal groups through the addition of modifiers ('a rather short, soft young fellow'). The phrase 'a true little Indian' is in apposition to the first long phrase, and performs the same function within the sentence – it would be part of the main clause if the sentence had one. Similarly, the two adverbial groups, 'in a rapid, low, musical voice' and 'with extraordinarily gentle intonation', both relate independently to the verb form 'speaking', which itself depends upon either the headword 'man' or the headword 'Indian'.

We have already seen qualifiers which are subordinate nominal groups introduced by a preposition – 'of dark-blue tiles', 'of painted wood' (*Three Novellas*, p. 163). When a grammatical item is dependent upon another item for its role in the sentence and could not make sense alone, or would make different sense alone, then that item is a subordinate group, or phrase, or clause. The two adverbial groups quoted above are co-ordinate with each other but subordinate to the verb 'speaking' which is in turn subordinate to the headword 'man' or 'Indian'. The connection between items of subordination is much more tightly controlled than between items of co-ordination, and is much more central to the logical thread of the sentence. (We shall see more of the value of co-ordination in writing when we come to look at Lawrence's poetry.) A fairly straightforward example is from the story 'The Man Who Loved Islands', written in June 1926: 'The islander moved himself, with all his books, into the commonplace six-roomed house up to which you had to scramble from the rocky landing-place.' (*Love Among the Haystacks and Other Stories*, p. 109) The main clause is 'The islander moved himself', and the group 'with all his books' is a subordinate nominal group introduced by a preposition and qualifying 'himself'. The phrase 'into the commonplace six-roomed house' is an adverbial group dependent upon the verb 'moved'. Then, 'up to which you had to scramble', which actually suggests the act of a difficult ascent in the awkwardness of its rhythm, is a subordinate clause, but one which depends upon the headword 'house' from the adverbial group. Finally, 'from the rocky landing-place' is also an adverbial group, introduced by a preposition, and relating to the verb 'scramble'. The subordinate groups do not all relate directly to the main clause, but are nevertheless controlled by it in that only the main clause is able to give the basic structure of the sentence that allows the subordinate clauses to expand upon and depend on each other in a logical succession. Together they are an amplification of the act of moving and of the effort and complexities involved.

A more complicated example will give some idea of the range of subordination that can be developed from a simple statement. The following sentence from 'Love Among the Haystacks', which is a very early story, consists of a main clause followed by a series of subordinate groups.

He washed himself from head to foot, standing in the fresh, forsaken corner of the field, where no one could see him by daylight, so that now, in the veiled grey tinge of moonlight, he was no more noticeable than the crowded flowers. (*Love Among the Haystacks and Other Stories*, p. 27)

The main clause in the sentence is 'He washed himself', followed by a subordinate adverbial group 'from head to foot' depending on the main verb 'washed'. The adverbial group 'standing in the fresh, forsaken corner of the field' also depends upon the verb 'washed'. However, the next clause, 'where no one could see him by daylight', depends not upon the main clause but upon the adverbial group 'standing in the fresh, forsaken corner of the field', and can be regarded as itself adverbial, relating to the verb form 'standing', or possibly as adjectival, depending upon the headword of the nominal group, 'the fresh, forsaken corner of the field', which is 'corner'. The adverbial clause 'so that now . . . he was no more visible than the crowded flowers' expresses a consequence not of the washing of the main clause but of where he is 'standing', and so also depends upon that subordinate adverbial group. Finally, 'in the veiled grey tinge of moonlight' is an adverbial group subordinate to the verb 'was' of the following clause, 'he was no more visible than the crowded flowers'. The sentence is rather unwieldy, and the patterns of subordination are complicated. The single fact related is that Maurice washed himself. At the same time the subordinate groups, only the first two of which are directly dependent upon the main clause, expand upon the fact of his washing to include the atmosphere and scene and even, by implication, something of his state of mind, so that we realise that the washing itself is less important than Lawrence's development of the feeling that is dependent on it. The main clause allows the subordinate groups to exist, and to that extent it controls them. But it is in fact outweighed by them in every respect but the grammatical. Again, Lawrence has thrown the grammatical arrangement of his writing awry in order to concentrate the reader's attention less upon the action itself, which is what attention to the grammatical focus of the sentence would require, and more upon those details of the circumstances that allow the mood and state of mind of the character to be inferred: isolation, quiet, the reminder of the day that has gone, darkness, moonlight, the richness and profusion of the flowers.

Some further briefer examples will demonstrate how Lawrence extends the range of dependence beyond that of conventional writing in English to include the relations between sentences. In *The Virgin and the Gipsy* there is the following paragraph:

The next day, at the party, she had no idea that she was being sweet to Leo. She had no idea that she was snatching him away from the tortured Ella Framley. Not until, when she was eating her pistachio ice, he said to her:

'Why don't you and me get engaged, Yvette?' (*St Mawr and The Virgin and the Gipsy*, p. 209)

The second sentence establishes a marked degree of continuity with the first by repeating the expression 'she had no idea' as its opening words. The third sentence, however, takes the continuity even further by actually depending on the second for its grammatical structure and its sense. The second is a complete expression in itself, but when read in the context of the third it too reveals its dependence insofar as it alters its meaning in the light of what are, in effect, later events. In fact, Lawrence has split the substance of a single sentence into two, but has preserved the dependence between the two halves, representing as they do the two stages of Yvette's mental process: she did not realise *until* Leo made his proposal. We see clearly the stages of the process, and see also, by the split, the gulf between the two. Yvette's innocence of the consequences is embodied in the grammatical structure, in a way that would not have been possible had the normal conventions prevailed.

Or Lawrence describes a market scene in *The Plumed Serpent*.

By the time the church bells clanged for sunset, the market had already begun. On all the pavements round the *plaza* squatted the Indians with their wares, pyramids of green water-melons, arrays of rough earthenware, hats in piles, pairs of sandals side by side, a great array of fruit, a spread of collar-studs and knick-knacks, called *novedades*, little trays with sweets. And people arriving all the time out of the wild country, with laden asses.

Yet never a shout, hardly a voice to be heard. None of the animation and the frank wild clamour of a Mediterranean market. Always the heavy friction of the will; always, always, grinding upon the spirit, like the grey black grind of lava-rock. (p. 243)

The relation here is predominantly one of co-ordination rather than subordination: the basic device is that of the list in which each item has an equal place. In this way the business and variety of the market is developed. Yet none of the sentences after the first two has a main verb, and so each depends upon an understood 'there were' or 'there was' – 'And *there were* people arriving', 'Yet *there was* never a shout'. Because Lawrence is actually interested not so much in the market but in the spirit of the people, the omission of main verbs and the dependence for meaning upon an absent understood verb is important in conveying grammatically the lack of spontaneity, the 'heavy friction of the will'.

In *St Mawr*, during the section in which he gives the history of Lou's ranch, Las Chivas, Lawrence extends the relatedness of sentences even further, to the patterning of his paragraphs. In the above example from *The Plumed Serpent* the reader is required to carry the 'there was' understood over from the first to the second paragraph in order to make sense of 'Yet never a shout, hardly a voice to be heard.' In *St Mawr* the dependence between paragraphs is more varied. The following sentences are mostly the last and first of succeeding paragraphs over some four pages of the book. The first character mentioned is the schoolmaster, the second the trader.

He made the long clearing for alfalfa.
And fell so into debt, that he had to trade his homestead away, to clear his debt.

After a number of years, he sent up the enamelled bath-tub to be put in the little log bath-house on the little wild ranch hung right against the savage Rockies, above the desert.
But here the mountains finished him.

All these things the trader could trade to the Mexicans, very advantageously.
And moreover, since somebody had started a praise of the famous goats' cheese made by Mexican peasants in New Mexico, goats there should be.
Goats there were: Ive hundred of them, eventually. . . . The Mexicans call them fire-mouths, because everything they nibble dies. Not because of their flaming mouths, really, but because they nibble a live plant down, down to the quick, till it can put forth no more.
So, the energetic trader, in the course of five or six years, had got the ranch ready.

The rats came, and the pack-rats, swarming.

And after all, it was difficult to sell or trade the cheeses, and little profit to be made. . . . In winter the goats scarcely drank at all. In summer they could be watered at the little spring. But the thirsty land was not so easy to accommodate.

Five hundred fine white Angora goats, with their massive handsome padres! . . . It was beautiful, and valuable, but comparatively little of it.

And it all cost, cost, cost. And a man was always let down. At one time no water. At another a poison-weed. Then a sickness. Always, some mysterious malevolence fighting, fighting against the will of man. (*St Mawr and The Virgin and the Gipsy*, pp. 148–51)

Throughout these extracts we see, as we have elsewhere, sentences depending for their main verbs upon previous sentences ('The Mexicans call them fire-mouths. . . . Not because of their flaming mouths . . . '). What is new is the degree to which Lawrence makes it impossible for each paragraph to be understood grammatically without taking over to it some linguistic item from a preceding one. The simplest examples involve straightforward co-ordination. 'And fell so into debt' has the same status as 'He made the long clearing', and really belongs to the same sentence. Yet not only are they different sentences but separate paragraphs. It is as if, in this world, the consequences of actions are further removed from the actions themselves than in conventional living. With 'But here the mountains finished him' we find a paragraph in which the opening qualifies the final sentence of the preceding paragraph, and in fact the whole paragraph: the trader's effort is expended, but finally is wasted and has to be reassessed in the light of the inevitable, if delayed, defeat by the mountains. Then the opening, 'So, the energetic trader', provides a summary of the activities of the preceding paragraphs, but in doing so manages to bear very little relation to the one immediately preceding, which deals with the habits of goats. The 'So' must be understood to refer much further back than a single paragraph. The key to this kind of paragraphing comes at the end of the quoted sequence. Organisation is the province of man's will, be it trying to run a ranch or write a passage of plain English. Working against this is the 'mysterious malevolence' which renders the efforts of the schoolmaster and the trader futile and requires that the language that describes its influence should depart from normal English and consist of sentences that are not true sentences, and of grammatical features that depend for their sense upon the linguistic happenings of previous paragraphs. 'Between the idea/And the reality/Between the motion/And the act/Falls the shadow',[2] writes T.S. Eliot in 'The Hollow Men', and the shadow that distorts his poetic language is also at work shaping the prose in this section of *St Mawr*.

The ways in which Lawrence makes items of language depend upon each other in his writing are often extreme and can make his work dense and, at times, ugly or opaque. Certainly, his language makes demands upon the reader that are not made by more conventional novelists, and these demands are as much in his handling of language as they are in the content of his novels. But one advantage, for a novelist whose intention is to 'reveal the relation between man and his circumambient universe, at the living moment' (*Phoenix*, p. 527), is that such writing displays in its very structure a high degree of relatedness. Events, objects, thoughts are felt to be in perpetual dialogue with each other, perpetually shifting in their relation to each other, as the grammatical structures that express them find new patterns of slightly modified meaning. Lawrence saw the need to develop a new language for the feelings in order to write the kind of fiction he felt was necessary. In doing so he also developed what might be termed a new grammar for the feelings, and one that demands a new kind of reader involvement. Writing for the feelings not only means providing the language in which a character's feelings can best be enacted. It requires that the feelings that are focused upon particular landscapes, or objects, or events are also given their clearest and most complete expression. And it means that both writer and reader will be impelled to relive those feelings through the medium of an English language that has been reinvented for the purpose.

This chapter has been concerned with the main features of Lawrence's use of language in prose, with the grammatical units deployed and some of the structures in which they can be arranged. At the same time I have tried to show, where possible, the reasons for the choices made in specific circumstances. What the next two chapters will do is to expand upon the basic features established here in order to demonstrate Lawrence's handling of language in creating a fictional context for dealing with certain topics – the world of the novels – and in developing characters and the relations between them.

5   Language in Use: the Fictional World

In his 1925 essay 'The Novel' Lawrence writes that 'In a novel, everything is relative to everything else, if that novel is art at all' (*Phoenix II*, 416). The main force of a Lawrence novel is always located in the characters, and his handling of character will be dealt with in the following chapter. But character cannot exist in isolation. Character, above all , must be related to 'everything else' in the novel if the novel is to be what Lawrence calls a 'quick' novel.

> The man in the novel must be "quick". And this means one thing, among a host of unknown meaning: it means he must have a quick relatedness to all the other things in the novel: snow, bed-bugs, sunshine, the phallus, trains, silk-hats, cats, sorrow, people, food, diphtheria, fuchsias, stars, ideas, God, tooth-paste, lightning, and toilet-paper. He must be in quick relation to all these things. What he says and does must be relative to them all. (*Phoenix II*, 420)

This is to say that in the novel we must be convinced that there is a living relationship between the characters and the circumstances of their being: the settings in which they appear, the actions in which they are engaged, the language they use and the language that is used of them. In the novel, says Lawrence, 'Everything is true in its own time, place, circumstance' (*Phoenix*, p. 528). What this chapter will be looking at is the ways Lawrence uses language to give the 'time, place, circumstance' in which it is possible for 'Everything' to be true.

One of the most immediately felt impressions for the reader

of a novel is the impact of a first or third person narrator. The achieving of a 'relatedness' within the novel begins with the relationship implied with the reader by each of these two modes of narration. Our trust as readers will be differently bestowed upon each. The 'I' narrator will need to make himself interesting or attractive in some way before we are prepared to give credit to his account. The third person narrator, however, depends far less on narrative personality and much more on the inherent qualities of what he is presenting. We have already seen something of Lawrence's attempts at first person narrative in *The White Peacock*, and the awkwardness of a narrator who is neither fully involved in the action nor ever able to be wholly apart from it. Lawrence occasionally returned to this mode in short stories ('The Fly in the Ointment', for example, first published in 1913, or 'One', first published in 1930), but for his major work, and especially for his novels, he had clearly decided that 'I' narrative did not afford the opportunities his kind of writing required. The reasons for this are not hard to find, for an 'I' narrator imposes severe limitations in both scope and language upon a writer. The main restriction concerns the necessity for coherence in the outlook and expression of someone who is supposedly a single individual with a life that is lived at the level of the characters in the book as well as an existence that relates to the lives of the readers. In fact, this restrictedness has made the first person narrator very suitable for exploitation in works intended to show up a particularly narrow or bizarre form of personality, such as Gulliver's in Swift's *Gulliver's Travels*, or Hilary Burde's in Iris Murdoch's *A Word Child*. But Lawrence is not interested in playing narrative games that trap either reader or character. At the same time, he requires the freedom to range over a variety of topics, some of them only obliquely relevant to his story, to see from a variety of perspectives, and to speak in a variety of linguistic forms. None of these would be possible without putting the greatest strains on a first person narrator. The 'I' of a Lawrence novel would very quickly appear either wholly inconsistent or quite mad, and any relationship achieved between writer and reader would be in ruins.

The twin advantages of third person narrative are the freedom from maintaining consistency of character and the perspective afforded by an omniscience that does not need to be justified.

Here, for example, is the opening of the story 'England, My England', which Lawrence wrote in June 1915, and which is set in the contemporary England of the First World War.

He was working on the edge of the common, beyond the small brook that ran in the dip at the bottom of the garden, carrying the garden path in continuation from the plank bridge on to the common. He had cut the rough turf and bracken, leaving the grey, dryish soil bare. But he was worried because he could not get the path straight, there was a pleat between his brows. He had set up his sticks, and taken the sights between the big pine trees, but for some reason everything seemed wrong. He looked again, straining his keen blue eyes, that had a touch of the Viking in them, through the shadowy pine trees as through a doorway, at the green-grassed garden-path rising from the shadow of alders by the log bridge up to the sunlit flowers. Tall white and purple columbines, and the butt-end of the old Hampshire cottage that crouched near the earth amid flowers, blossoming in the bit of shaggy wildness round about. (*England, My England*, p. 7)

This is a relatively low-key opening, especially when compared with the opening of *The Rainbow*, which dates from the same period of Lawrence's writing. The main intention is to establish the character of Egbert and the setting for the story, and the sentences are steady and methodical in their laying down of scene and circumstance. The first two sentences, for example, present us with the man's work prior to telling anything about him as an individual at all. The contours of the garden are known in more detail than Egbert at this stage, and the work that has already taken place is brought to our attention before the man who has carried it out. Only with the third sentence do we get a focus on Egbert with the two co-ordinate clauses ('he was worried . . . ' and 'there was a pleat . . . ') that tell of the worry he is feeling. The immediate history of this worry is then inserted, followed by his present action, his 'looking again', as a consequence of that worry. This looking is then used as an opportunity to give something of the appearance of the scene as a whole, which includes the house where Egbert lives. In these respects, there is nothing particularly unusual about the passage.

Yet Lawrence in fact allows himself considerable liberty in terms of presentation, not least in his manipulation of sentence structure in order to develop the kind of person Egbert will turn out to be. It is noticeable, for example, that the garden and its surroundings are more forcefully reflected in the structure of the sentences than Egbert himself is. In the first sentence, two of the three verb forms are concerned with Egbert, 'was working' and 'carrying', yet they are almost lost sight of under the detail of the setting that Lawrence packs into the sentence structure. The adverbial group 'beyond the small brook . . . ' that depends upon 'working' in fact outweighs the verb altogether by virtue of its length, including a dependent verbal group, 'ran', and the apparently endless string of dependent nominal groups, 'in the dip at the bottom of the garden'. One effect of this may be to suggest the continuousness of the running of the brook, but the more important consequence is that our first experience of Egbert is of the ineffectiveness of his labour in the face of the permanence of the lie of the land. It is, in fact, only by an effort of attention that we then realise that the verb 'carrying' actually refers back to Egbert's 'working' and is telling us just what it is he is doing. Again, it is the work itself that we see, and only subsequently are we invited to connect the work with an intention and therefore with an intelligence capable of forming and holding to intention. As if in irony, the 'pleat' between Egbert's brows reflects the straightness he is unsuccessfully attempting to achieve as he looks at the path, while 'his keen blue eyes' can see clearly what he is trying to do without making him able to do it. Perhaps the biggest surprise in the paragraph, though, is the adjectival clause 'that had a touch of the Viking in them'. The very expression, a 'touch' of the 'Viking', almost suggests a contradiction in terms, for our associations with Vikings do not normally include anything so delicate as a 'touch'. As with his work, Egbert is at the 'edge' of his inheritance. His ancestry, like his capacity for achievement, is a mere hint made slightly ludicrous by the remorseless intractability of present reality. And as he looks 'through the shadowy pine trees' that come between him and his surroundings, between him and his ancestry, him and what he sees, like a 'doorway', he looks at a prospect that presents itself as more secure, as more completely fulfilled as itself than he can hope to be: the comfortable 'green-grassed garden-path', the 'sunlit flowers', the 'tall' columbines and the 'old' cottage. In the last sentence in particular neither of the two verb forms, 'crouched' and 'blossoming', is the main verb. These details of what Egbert sees are able to assert their existence in a sentence that has no need of a main verb, because they just *are*.

A few pages later Lawrence describes Egbert's relations with his own family. He is 'out of it. Without anything happening, he was gradually, unconsciously excluded from the circle.' (*England, My England*, p. 14) We can read the preparations for this from the opening sentence of the story, not only in what is told us, with Egbert found 'on the edge of the common', but in the structures of the sentences themselves that embody an attitude towards the character on the part of the third person narrator. By the second paragraph, in fact, when in most stories we might expect the focus to shift to the mind of the character who is being established, we find that the sense impressions that are introduced are responded to not by Egbert but by the unexpectedly strong opinions of the narrator.

> There was a sound of children's voices calling and talking: high, childish, girlish voices, slightly didactic and tinged with domineering: 'If you don't come quick, nurse, I shall run out there to where there are snakes.' And nobody had the *sang-froid* to reply: 'Run then, little fool.' It was always, 'No, darling. Very well, darling. In a moment, darling. Darling, you *must* be patient.' (*England, My England*, p. 7)

Because we later discover that it is Egbert who is in fact responsible for his children's being spoilt, it clearly cannot be his critical reflection that would say 'Run then, little fool.' Lawrence himself, requiring the criticism to be made but unable to make it through his main character, has for a moment taken over as the leading personality in his own work, has broken cover in order to inject a strength and a directness that are lacking in Egbert. And again, the language is thereby made to work against the character, for the direct spech of 'Run then, little fool' and the mimicked 'Very well, darling' are quite contrary to the language that deals with Egbert, getting lost in 'the shadow of alders by the log bridge' or vaguely wondering why 'for some reason everything seemed wrong'. The very device of breaking into the narrative is itself a shock that runs counter to the mode of expression that is suitable for the story of Egbert, and it is, of course, a shock that could not have been achieved had Lawrence chosen a first instead of a third person narrator.

Even in a fairly straightforward passage, then, we can see some of the advantages of third person narrative, and the kind of exploitation of language and reader expectation that Lawrence finds necessary for the writing of his kind of fiction. At the same time, it is apparent that in the setting of a fictional world, Lawrence is doing more than providing a background against which his characters will be placed, for not only is setting integral to character but the language of setting is itself a factor in the overall impact made by the novel or story. And if circumstance must be made true to character, so too must the language in which circumstance is rendered be true to the purpose the fiction has set out to achieve.

Description is clearly one important aspect of the fictional world created by the novelist, and descriptive writing can bring out a variety of tones and methods depending on the reason for the description's being in the novel at all. At the beginning of *St Mawr*, for example, there are several paragraphs describing the relationship between Lou Witt and Rico and their present life style. Here the tone is quite different from either 'England, My England' or *The Rainbow*, for Lawrence is clearly adopting the language of the trivial social set to which Lou and Rico belong.[1]

Lou Witt had had her own way so long, that by the age of twenty-five she didn't know where she was. Having one's own way landed one completely at sea.

To be sure for a while she had failed in her grand love affair with Rico. And then she had had something really to despair about. But even that had worked out as she wanted. Rico had come back to her, and was dutifully married to her. And now, when she was twenty-five and he was three months older, they were a charming married couple. He flirted with other women still, to be sure. He wouldn't be the handsome Rico if he didn't. But she had 'got' him. Oh yes! You had only to see the uneasy backward glance at her, from his big blue eyes: just like a horse that is edging away from its master: to know how completely he was mastered. (*St Mawr and The Virgin and the Gipsy*, p. 11)

The casually colloquial inelegance of the first sentences – 'had had her own way so long', 'she didn't know where she was', 'landed one completely at sea' – establishes the tone and, more significantly, the values that characterise this life style. The lazy omissions ('so long' instead of 'for so long'), the mechanical repetitions ('to be sure'), the self-consciously adopted clichés ('charming married couple'), the thoughtlessly brief sentences, all indicate language that is being used from a perspective of leisured indolence. (Interestingly, the same mechanical phrase, 'to be sure', is used to establish quite a different social setting at the beginning of the story 'You Touched Me': 'To be sure, a privet hedge partly masked the house and its ground. . . . '(*England, My England*, p. 107) Here the tone is taken from the world of the unmarried daughters of a respectable Midlands pottery owner.) Only at the end of the second paragraph in *St Mawr* is there a marked change of tone, in preparation for the quite different style and language when Lawrence turns to describe the horse some eight pages later. There is still repetition, but it is the more characteristic Lawrentian repetition which involves returning again and again to a term in order to establish, modify and re-establish its significance for the characters and the story. So, here Rico is referred to in terms of his 'master', and then, in a shift from nominal to verbal group, is described as 'mastered'. The sentence, too, displays not the casually thrown together quality of the rest of the paragraph, but actually works in its construction to enact the 'edging' of the horse and man. The heavy punctuation that separates out the 'horse' comparison and disrupts the flow of the sense between 'You had only to see' and 'to know' builds uneasiness into the sentence as well as a kind of suppressed and unpredictable energy. And indeed such energy breaks out later in the story, both with St Mawr's throwing Rico and with Rico's unexpected resolution to have the horse gelded.

The opening description of 'England, My England' is governed by the kind of character Lawrence is intending to establish, while the opening of *St Mawr* takes its tone more from a social group that has largely formed the characters that are to be the subject of the story. The story itself deals with the development of a spiritual awareness in Lou and her gradual discarding of the values and assumptions of her background. Most of Lawrence's main characters are endowed with two spheres of existence: the life within, that is explored and developed as the novel or story progresses, and a life as a member of a social group that frequently has strong conventions and traditions, and strong linguistic forms, and is consequently resistant to change. In terms of presentation, the inner development of character, as we shall see, tends to be rendered through narrative description. Indeed, there is often a problem for Lawrence in overcoming the gap between his characters' emotional experiences and their inadequacies in articulacy that inhibit their coming to terms with those experiences. This means that the reader is generally given a more coherent account of emotional events than is available to the character him or herself. But when Lawrence presents social life, his method tends far more towards letting people speak and act for themselves, using the language to which they have access and working within the restrictions of the social group with which he is dealing.

Mrs Morel, in *Sons and Lovers*, is a woman of some refinement and education, with a consciousness of her own superiority over the other families of her neighbourhood. She is also a strong influence on Paul's tastes and his expectations in life. In a revealing scene, Lawrence portrays her public life as a miner's wife receiving news of an accident at the pit.

About a year after William went to London, and just after Paul had left school before he got work, Mrs Morel was upstairs and her son was painting in the kitchen – he was very clever with his brush – when there came a knock at the door. Crossly he put down his brush to go. At the same moment his mother opened a window upstairs and looked down.

A pit-lad in his dirt stood on the threshold.

'Is this Walter Morel's?' he asked.

'Yes,' said Mrs Morel. 'What is it?'

But she had guessed already.

'Your mester's got hurt,' he said.

'Eh, dear me!' she exclaimed. 'It's a wonder if he hadn't, lad. And what's he done this time?'

'I don't know for sure, but it's 'is leg somewhere. They ta'ein' 'im ter th' 'ospital.'

'Good gracious me!' she exclaimed. 'Eh, dear, what a one he is! There's not five minutes of peace. I'll be hanged

if there is! His thumb's nearly better, and now – – Did you
see him?'

'I seed him at th' bottom. An' I seed 'em bring 'im up in
a tub, an' 'e wor in a dead faint. But he shouted like anythink
when Doctor Fraser examined him i' th' lamp cabin – an' cossed
an' swore, an' said as 'e wor gon' to be ta'en whoam – 'e worn't
goin' ter th' 'ospital.'

The boy faltered to an end.

'He *would* want to come home, so that I can have all the
bother. Thank you, my lad. Eh, dear, if I'm not sick – sick
and surfeited, I am!'

She came downstairs. Paul had mechanically resumed his
painting. (*Sons and Lovers*, p. 106)

What is remarkable here is the strikingly different levels of expression that are made available to the reader. There is first of all the
language of the third person narrator, providing a recognisable
version of 'normal' English. But this norm is suddenly exposed
to the extreme, sometimes almost unrecognisable English of the
pit-lad. Not only is his use of language distorted by Lawrence's
deployment of apostrophes and non-standard spelling ('whoam')
to indicate his pronunciation. The structure of his grammar is
also at variance with the narrative norm. 'They ta'ein' 'im ter
th' 'ospital', for example, turns out to be the lad's version of the
continuous present, 'they are taking', with the auxiliary omitted,
though at first sight the missing auxiliary appears to be 'have',
and the sense to be 'they have taken', the present perfect. And
'seed' is the simple past 'saw'. The expression 'an' said as' is the
idiomatic for 'and said that'. The word 'wor' is particularly interesting in that it is a version of the simple past, 'were',[2] but is used
indiscriminately whenever the past of the verb 'to be' is required,
including occasions when the normal usage would be 'was' – 'he
was in a dead faint'. But one of the things the passage, and others
like it in *Sons and Lovers*, makes us aware of is that such usage
is the norm for the world in which the novel is set. To the pit-lad
and everyone like him in 'Bestwood' it would be the voice of the
narrator that was out of place. One version of English, in other
words, and one that many of us as readers recognise as 'normal',
is being held up against a second version that is equally 'normal'
for those who speak it. The Lawrence who is telling the story

would be as 'non-standard' at the pit as the lad is outside of his own neighbourhood.

Paul himself has no dialogue during the passage, but this is significant. We know from elsewhere in the novel that Paul is not a speaker of Standard English ('They always stan' in front of me, so's I can't get out' (p. 93)), though he is critical of the language of his neighbours ('Mr Braithwaite drops his "h's", an' Mr Winterbottom says "You was".' (p. 93)). Here, having nothing to say means that he is incorporated through the descriptions of his actions, and through his role as an overhearer, into the norm of the narrator and remains outside, therefore, the world of the pit and its linguistic norms. 'Paul had mechanically resumed painting' strikes a particularly mannered note, with the educated 'resumed' chosen in preference to a more colloquial 'carried on' or even 'started painting again'. He has no part of this world or its language, as we have already seen when as a younger boy he is sent to collect his father's wages. His small voice is not heard by the cashier and Paul, 'suffering convulsions of self-consciousness', cannot call out again. The cashier's brusque question, 'Why don't you shout up when you're called?' (p. 91) is the counterpart to 'The boy faltered to a halt.' Both Paul and the pit-lad have found themselves in situations in which their linguistic competence is inadequate, or out of place, and the most natural haven for each of them is silence. It is worth noting that after the lad's departure, Mrs Morel's first speech to Paul includes the rather impatient order, 'Put those things away, there's no time to be painting now' (p. 107), as if rejecting his world of more refined tastes and activities – a world to which she has introduced him – in favour of the world conveyed by the pit-lad's message. The world of dialect and public duty must come first, and Paul's world, associated with taste, self-expression and articulacy, is put aside as a luxury, almost as self-indulgence.

It is Mrs Morel's dialogue, however, that is most revealing. She speaks from the upstairs window, a whole world apart from the behavioural norms of Mrs Beardsall, Lawrence's earlier portrayal of his mother in *The White Peacock*. Initially, the pit-lad's 'Your mester' jars with the reader, for 'master' is exactly what Walter Morel is not, in his wife's eyes. The word is a good example of how social values are inseparable from colloquial expression, for 'mester' is a version of both 'master' and 'mister'[3] which in today's usage have different implications. The lad, in saying 'your husband's been hurt', is endorsing the system of values in which the husband is acknowledged as master of his home and family. Yet Mrs Morel apparently accepts the word, and responds in a style that is far closer to the lad's than it is to the language of the narrator: 'Eh, dear me! . . . It's a wonder if he hadn't, lad.' The structure of her remark is no more standard than dropping 'h's' and saying 'You was'. 'It would have been a wonder if he hadn't' is the 'normal' English version of what she says, which uses the conditional perfect continuous form of the verb 'to be', for which Mrs Morel substitutes the simple present 'is'. She employs colloquial expressions as well as structures: 'I'll be hanged if there is!' and 'if I'm not sick – sick and surfeited'. In fact Mrs Morel is confirmed by the passage not as the lady of superior upbringing who is moulding her son into a better man than his father, but as someone who slips easily into the role of the miner's wife in the time-honoured scene of receiving the news from the pit. She is worried, complaining, resigned. But most of all she is linguistically at home in the scene and it is Paul who is implicitly shunned as the outsider, the character with no role who idles away his time painting and associating himself with Standard English. She reverts to the type required by her social position, and turns against her own creation, the son who has no social position.

This reading of the passage, of course, goes against the grain of the novel, for she does not consciously hold these opinions, and Lawrence does not intend her to take this position. Indeed, as she goes off to see her husband she 'felt at the back of her, her son's heart waiting on her, felt him bearing what part of the burden he could, even supporting her' (p. 108). What is demonstrated, though, is the extent to which characters depend on a firmly established social setting for their 'true' existence, and how completely their behaviour and values must arise out of the norms expected by that society. The story is Paul's, and he therefore occupies a privileged position with respect to the narrative voice. The narrator's articulacy is largely expended in opening up Paul's emotional and spiritual development. Other characters, not least Mrs Morel, are developed more through being seen as *part* of their social context, rather than *against* it, as Paul is. And this, as demonstrated, has clear implications for the language that is used by and of each one of them.

The language of social groups, then, is used by Lawrence both in the creation of setting and in the development of character, and the groups portrayed are drawn from many levels and kinds of society: farming communities, as in *The Rainbow* or 'Love Among the Haystacks'; factory life, in *Sons and Lovers*; the military world, as with Anton Skrebensky in *The Rainbow*, or in stories like 'The Prussian Officer', 'The Thorn in the Flesh' and 'The Captain's Doll'; polite and even effete society, in the Cafe Pompadour 'set' in *Women in Love*, or the Manbys in *St Mawr*; or the lives of Indians, Mexicans, aborigines and primitive peoples of various kinds, as found in *St Mawr*, *The Plumed Serpent*, *Kangaroo*, *The Woman Who Rode Away*, and many other works. But if the language of groups is used to establish the 'truth' of the fictional world, it is also handled in a way that reveals the narrowness of group outlook, and this too is part of the 'truth' of circumstances. The strength an individual finds in being unquestioningly part of a social group is that he or she is supported by an unthinking acceptance in every act or speech of his or her life. Even Nut-Nat, the cretin who sells nuts around the public-houses in *The Rainbow*, is accepted by the men as having a role within the social group, until the girl Anna Brangwen, asserting her right to individual judgement, pronounces him 'a *horrid* man' and their support is gradually withdrawn (p. 89). The price to be paid for such support, of course, is to share the shortcomings of group perspective and to sacrifice the right that Anna as a child can assert, the right to cultivate one's individuality. It is this right that Ursula Brangwen, Paul Morel, Rupert Birkin, Lou Witt, Connie Chatterley, and of course D. H. Lawrence, decide is their first duty as living, thinking human beings, and this naturally means that they are brought into conflict with group values, the group outlook on life, and the language of group thought and expression.

The advantages and disadvantages of group membership are particularly concentrated in the question of group language. In a highly restricted linguistic register, such as the pit-lad's, the range of structures will be narrow and the variety of topics available for discussion very limited. At the same time, the slightest variation in sound will have a meaning that is readily understood by other users of that register. The same is true in a register that includes a high proportion of slang, or jargon: many shades of meaning, or of humour, will be communicated to initiates, and nothing at all to anyone else. Simply to understand, and to be expected by other group members to understand and to reply in kind, is a signal of acceptance, or personal validation, for the individual member. To take an oath of confirmation, as in joining a religious group, or a freemason's lodge, or the Wolf Cubs, is not only to promise acceptance of certain values: it is to put into words one's linguistic competence in attaching certain values to certain kinds of language ('the power and the glory', 'dyb dyb dyb'). Naturally, though, the acceptance of certain values means the exclusion of other values, and the enshrinement of values in the texture and structure of group language means that those excluded values can be neither spoken of nor contemplated: linguistically, they will not exist.[4] Part of the quest of Paul or Ursula is to rediscover that which has not existed, and their doing so necessarily involves turning aside from the language of the group and becoming more closely associated with the more flexible, if less predictable, language of the third person narrator.

Because in Lawrence the social background is never just background, the narrowness imposed by group membership is a significant feature of making the 'truth' of the fictional world, and it is a truth which incorporates some characters wholly, and to which others 'relate' through the act of rebellion. Indeed, the nature of their rebellion is partly governed by their assessment of what it is they are rebelling against, of its values and linguistic norms. In the following passage from *The Rainbow*, Ursula as a teenager, with her schoolmistress/lover, Winifred Inger, are visiting Ursula's Uncle Tom Brangwen, an educated and much travelled man who is now a colliery manager in Wiggiston. They are about to take tea. The passage is long, but does demonstrate well the relationship of four separate characters to the social and linguistic norm that is the background to much of the second half of the novel.

'I suppose their lives are not really so bad,' said Winifred Inger, superior to the Zolaesque tragedy.

He turned with his polite, distant attention.

'Yes, they are pretty bad. The pits are very deep, and hot, and in some places wet. The men die of consumption fairly often. But they earn good wages.'

'How gruesome!' said Winifred Inger.

'Yes,' he replied gravely. It was his grave, solid, self-contained manner which made him so much respected as a colliery manager.

The servant came in to ask where they would have tea.

'Put it in the summer-house, Mrs Smith,' he said.

The fair-haired, good-looking young woman went out.

'Is she married and in service?' asked Ursula.

'She is a widow. Her husband died of consumption a little while ago.' Brangwen gave a sinister little laugh. 'He lay there in the house-place at her mother's, and five or six other people in the house, and died very gradually. I asked her if his death wasn't a great trouble to her. "Well," she said, "he was very fretful towards the last, never satisfied, never easy, always fretting, an' never knowing what would satisfy him. So in one way it was a relief when it was over – for him and for everybody." They had only been married two years, and she has one boy. I asked her if she hadn't been very happy. "Oh, yes, sir, we was very comfortable at first, till he took bad, – oh, we was very comfortable, – oh, yes – but, you see, you get used to it. I've had my father and two brothers go off just the same. You get used to it." '

'It's a horrible thing to get used to,' said Winifred Inger, with a shudder.

'Yes,' he said, still smiling. 'But that's how they are. She'll be getting married again directly. One man or another – it does not matter very much. They're all colliers.'

'What do you mean?' asked Ursula. 'They're all colliers?'

'It is with the women as with us,' he replied. 'Her husband was John Smith, loader. We reckoned him as a loader, he reckoned himself as a loader, and so she knew he represented his job. Marriage and home is a little side-show. The women know it right enough, and take it for what it's worth. One man or another, it doesn't matter all the world. The pit matters. Round the pit there will always be the side-shows, plenty of 'em.' (pp. 348–9)

The character here who is most completely incorporated within the social norms is Mrs Smith, who significantly has no direct speech of her own during the passage. Her story is related by Tom, who does, however, quote her directly for much of his speech, which enables us to assess the extent to which her social assumptions and expectations are bound and defined by her linguistic norms. Her range of vocabulary is narrow, and this is emphasised by Lawrence's making her repeat herself in the lines that are reported: 'comfortable' twice, 'get used to it' twice, both 'fretful' and 'satisfied' used once as adjective and once as verb. So, too, are the linguistic structures she employs: the string of complements after the verb 'was': 'very fretful . . . never satisfied . . . never easy . . . always fretting . . . never knowing'; the disruptions in the last few sentences of repeated structures: 'oh, yes . . . we was very comfortable . . . you get used to it'. The most distinctive feature of her language, though, is the words that are clearly *not* distinctive within the social group to which she belongs. Words like 'fretful', 'took bad' and 'go off' are the time-honoured terms for becoming ill and dying, as 'comfortable' is for being happy. And if to 'go off' or to be 'comfortable' restricts one from experiencing the deep grief of bereavement or the exhilaration of utter bliss, they also protect one from emotional exposure to either of these extremes. The traditional words impart a representative value to experience: they sustain the individual by making her, or his, pleasures and pains stand for the community's. At the same time the individual goes through nothing that has not been gone through by preceding generations, who have passed down the terms to deal with marriage, sickness and bereavement, terms that help you 'get used to it'. Mrs Smith's use of the second person pronoun is indicative: she does not personalise the experience by saying 'I've got used to it', but distances it and in so doing generalises it into one of life's norms, for her 'you' does not refer to Tom Brangwen to whom she is speaking, but to all the men and women in her community who have suffered over the years and who will suffer in the future. She has come to terms with the death, was even, as we can see, coming to terms with it before it happened ('very fretful towards the last, never satisfied . . . a relief when it was over'), and in a large measure her coming to terms is made inevitable by the language she has used in speaking and thinking about the event. She is sustained by it, wholly absorbed in it, and to that extent her outlook is narrowed by it at the same time that she is protected.

Uncle Tom is in a different position. He is responsible for

enfolding Mrs Smith's language in his own, just as he takes responsibility as colliery manager for the welfare and efficiency of the entire mining community of the neighbourhood. He is outside her language and assumptions, but as his language makes clear he also largely shares those assumptions even while he is describing them. He speaks a steady, measured, unemotional kind of English, rational and uncritical. His description of the hardships of pit life in his first speech is straightforwardly factual. But the conditions, that would otherwise speak for themselves, are given a strange twist by his casual phrases 'pretty bad' and 'fairly often'. It is as if Tom is fully aware of the horrors of the employment he supervises but somehow is capable of playing them down in his own mind, especially as the men 'earn good wages'. He too has come to terms with something, but in his case it is other people's suffering that he has accepted, not his own. This is one perspective on his 'self-contained manner'. He is impersonal, accepts things as they are, makes no demands for change, either through what he is prepared to say or in the way he says it. His story of Mrs Smith's life is told without comment and only in answer to Ursula's question. The only moral he is willing to draw from it is 'that's how they are', where the personal pronoun, in careful contrast to Mrs Smith's, gives the impression that 'they' are somehow a different species of life to us here, Tom and Ursula Brangwen, Winifred Inger. The feelings that 'normal' educated people like us have are dulled, or absent, in them.

And yet everything Tom says shows that he is himself quite without an emotional dimension to his life. If Mrs Smith and her late husband accepted the 'reckoning' of 'John Smith, loader', it was because they had no choice: their whole background and language gave them no option. With Tom, he has the choice because he understands the system of mechanisation that makes for the incorporation of men into their function, and he has chosen to support it. The making of that choice is what has shown him to be as trapped by the system as the people he manages, and his lack of emotional capacity is reflected not in a narrowness of linguistic range and the use of a restricted idiom, but in the one-dimensional quality of his language. 'It is with the women as with us. . . . Her husband was John Smith, loader. We reckoned him as a loader, he reckoned himself as a loader, and so she knew he represented his job.' His 'us' and

'We' confirm the separation he perceives between the mining community and the educated managerial class, but at the same time he is unconsciously displaying his own willingness to become 'representative': not 'I' Tom Brangwen 'reckoned him' but 'we' the mine for whose corporate mentality I stand. And his speech has as much repetition as Mrs Smith's, though it is of a different order. Here it is of key terms, 'loader', and 'reckoned', and of the structures of his assertions which leave no room for other ways of saying it: pronoun or noun, verb, complement. This is, of course, the fundamental structure of statements in English. What is so unusual in Tom's speech is the lack of elaboration on the basic structure and the apparently deliberate avoiding of any variation from it, any resourceful exploitation of the opportunities afforded by grammatical or rhythmic change. Over and over again he simply asserts, usually employing the verb to be: 'They are pretty bad', 'The pits are very deep', 'they earn good wages', 'She is a widow', 'she has one boy', 'Marriage and home is a little side-show', 'They're all colliers'. The mechanisation that he has accepted for other people's lives has entered the structure of his own language, and he has given up the flexibility afforded by linguistic variety which enables a fully alert individual to be emotionally alive as well as intellectually competent. The language to which he has restricted himself excludes the possibility of his being open to the values of humane feeling, just as Mrs Smith's language prevents her from challenging the awfulness of her lot by restricting her capacity to grasp values that would give any meaning to her challenge.

It is noticeable that Tom is only named once during the passage, even though he does most of the talking. Usually he is the impersonal 'he'. Winifred, on the other hand, is given her full name each time she has something to say. She and Ursula are in the position of the reader, coming for the first time close to the colliery world that has gradually been encroaching upon the farming world of the earlier generations of Brangwens. Winifred, the schoolteacher, is anxious to let the measure of her concern show upon the surface of her language ('How gruesome!' and 'It's a horrible thing to get used to'), though initially looking for some extenuating circumstances, some reason for not attempting to confront the emotion she feels she ought to feel ('I suppose their lives are not really so bad'). The little that Winifred says displays the inadequacy of her emotions and her language in approaching genuine hardship. Like Tom, she has the intellectual capacity to know that hardship exists, and unlike him she does not yet wish to render herself inured to it. But, as signalled by the narrator in the rather surprising nominal group 'the Zolaesque tragedy', her norms are those of an educated middle class whose exposure to suffering is through literature. As such, she can only come out with banal exclamations in which she attempts to find terms sufficiently serious to convey the emotions she ought to feel – 'gruesome' and 'horrible'. Her being afforded her full name each time is a measure of her self-consciousness, of being who she is in this unusual situation with the linguistic equipment at her disposal when in fact she is much more at ease in the restricted world where 'I suppose' and 'How gruesome!' are perfectly adequate terms of response.

The contrast with Ursula is striking. She has already argued that the pits and her Uncle Tom are wrong: 'You think like they do – that living human beings must be taken and adapted to all kinds of horrors. We could easily do without the pits.' (p. 347) In the above passage, her only form of speech is the question. She challenges both the system Tom describes and the linguistic forms he uses to make sense of it. She does not, like Winifred, attempt to find a polite but adequate response in its own terms, because for Ursula there is no adequate response. She is referred to each time simply as Ursula, for her presence is not the self-conscious presence of the out-of-place Winifred Inger. Rather, she is there as a fully responding individual, owing no allegiance to the system she sees imposed but feeling keenly the suffering it inflicts on human beings who should have the right she is asserting to an individual judgement, an individual challenge. Her questions, especially the very direct affront of 'What do you mean? . . . They're all colliers?', assault the system that Tom is describing, but more than this they strike at the structural basis of his language. The mechanical assertions are suddenly made to justify themselves by a quite different grammatical arrangement, whereas Winifred Inger's response to the same story actually adopts Tom's own sentence structure of pronoun, verb, complement: 'It's a horrible thing. . . . ' Ursula's use of the personal pronoun, 'you', in 'What do you mean?', unlike Mrs Smith's use, does, of course, mean you Tom Brangwen. But Tom's linguistic resilience is unassailable, and the same mechanical pattern reasserts itself without flinching: 'It is with the women as with us. . . . Her husband was John Smith, loader. . . . ' But Ursula's challenge has presented an alternative, albeit briefly. She has shown that an individual can stand outside the system and from that position be inside the suffering that those who are trapped are scarcely conscious of any more. Ursula is the only one of these four characters whose language is expressed from a sense of her own individuality, as opposed to arising from a set of norms more or less imposed by unconscious acceptance of a social system. And if this enables her to mount a rebellion against these norms, it also impels her expression of a reaction that arises from no predetermined structures of emotion or language, but from common humanity.

In this sense, Ursula, like Paul Morel, Connie Chatterley, Lou Witt and other characters in rebellion, is the figure in *The Rainbow* most closely associated with the values of the narrator and, therefore, with Lawrence's intentions in writing fiction. Ursula is herself finding out the way to 'live', to bring herself 'into being' (*Phoenix*, p. 410). Her experimentation and unpredictability in this search are matched by the narrator's own. We have seen in *St Mawr* how Lawrence can adopt one kind of language for the opening of a work, only to move into a quite different range a few pages later. So, the voice that opens *The Rainbow* in strong poetic, even Biblical, fashion can describe the simple details of a child's relationship with its parent, the complex sourness of a relationship that is going bad, or, most surprisingly, can enter upon a lengthy harangue of one of his main characters, written in the language of social theory.

> He could not see, it was not born in him to see, that the highest good of the community as it stands is no longer the highest good of even the average individual. He thought that, because the community represents millions of people, therefore it must be millions of times more important than any individual, forgetting that the community is an abstraction from the many, and is not the many themselves. Now when the statement of the abstract good for the community has become a formula lacking in all inspiration or value to the average intelligence, then the 'common good' becomes a general nuisance, representing the vulgar, conservative materialism at a low level. (p. 329)

This is a discursive passage, and its style depends on a high density of nominal groups in which the headwords tend to be abstract nouns and the modifiers to describe abstract qualities: 'the highest good', 'the community', 'the average individual', 'an abstraction', 'the many', 'the average intelligence', 'the vulgar, conservative materialism'. Needless to say, this makes for very dull reading, and the verbal groups, being largely functional and colourless ('stands', 'is', 'represents', 'has become'), do not alleviate the dullness. What is said here has very little to do with character development. In fact, most of it actually expands on what the character, Anton Skrebensky, is said to be incapable of seeing. Its validity as social theory, too, may be open to question. But its contribution to the fictional world is significant in so far as Lawrence, like Ursula in the visit to Wiggiston, is engaged in disrupting accepted norms. He is ensuring that his voice does not become predictable, and that the fictional norms that he establishes – the settings, the values that the characters adhere to, the relationship between character and social group, the language that conveys the world of the novel to the reader – can never be taken for granted. The world of Lawrence's fiction is one that can at any time be challenged by the narrator himself, who is capable of exploring any subject that seizes his imagination, or of adopting a style of language that would seem to be at odds with the normal conventions of English fiction.

This, for Lawrence, is as it should be. For fiction to do its job properly, it cannot allow either the narrator or the reader to grow torpid in the telling of a tale that has become conventional. If the central character of a Lawrence novel is not permitted to take things for granted, no more can the writer himself. Lawrence's conception of what fiction should be doing changed, as we have seen, during his career, and the language used to develop the fictional world changed correspondingly, but he retained as part of his practice the willingness to go outside the limits of ordinary writing. He was, in other words, constantly alert to the necessity to shock if his conception of the novel as a dynamic form was to be realised.

What this chapter has shown is that while it is possible to isolate some of the means by which Lawrence creates a fictional world – kind and style of narration, the language of description, the language of kinds of society, and the readiness to disrupt – it is difficult to discuss setting and background without also talking about character. In particular, the use of language in fiction cannot ultimately be separated from the characters who for much of the narration are required to use and relate to that language. In Chapter 6, the focus will shift to character itself, to Lawrence's conception of character and to the implications this has for the language of his fiction.

6 Language in Use: Men and Women

> The great relationship, for humanity, will always be the relation between man and woman. The relation between man and man, woman and woman, parent and child, will always be subsidiary.
>
> And the relation between man and woman will change for ever, and will for ever be the new central clue to human life. It is the *relation itself* which is the quick and the central clue to life, not the man, nor the woman, nor the children that result from the relationship, as a contingency.
>
> It is no use thinking you can put a stamp on the relation between man and woman, to keep it in the *status quo*. You can't. You might as well try to put a stamp on the rainbow or the rain. (*Phoenix*, p. 531)

This is from 'Morality and the Novel', one of the essays Lawrence wrote in June 1925, and sets out clearly what is at the core of his interests as a writer. Characteristically, he writes with some force of the delicacy of the relations between man and woman. Yet his practice, over the years of his major fiction, in exploring and developing the complexities and inconsistencies of the loves between his characters shows both subtlety in understanding and technical skill in the use of language to convey, without 'stamping', the nuances of the 'great relationship'. At the same time, he uncharacteristically understates his interest in and assessment of the 'lesser' relationships in his work. Few readers would regard the friendship between Gerald and Birkin in *Women in Love* as 'subsidiary' to the love between Birkin and Ursula, and perhaps not as a lesser artistic achievement either. Certainly, the relations between the first Tom Brangwen and his step-daughter Anna, and between Will and his daughter Ursula, are among the most convincing and telling parts of *The Rainbow*, and are as 'quick' in their way as the relations between Will and Anna, or Ursula and Anton Skrebensky, which are much more fully treated.

In any fictional relationship, however, it is not enough to portray only the way that characters relate to each other, though that is clearly the end that Lawrence sets himself. First of all, each character, to be read as a 'quick' character, must be seen to relate to him or herself, or to be failing to do so in a way that is part of his or her quickness.

One of Lawrence's best-known statements on his conception of character was written in June 1914 from Italy in a letter to Edward Garnett. At that time the relationship between Garnett and himself was nearing its end and Garnett's influence was already passing. The year 1914 was one of rapid development for Lawrence. He had been living with Frieda since May 1912 and was working on the novel that was to become *The Rainbow*. Through Frieda he had become acquainted with new ideas, not least those associated with Freud and with psychoanalysis, and his living on the continent, and in Italy particularly, had brought him closer to European Modernism and experimentalism, most notably to the work of Filippo Marinetti and the Futurists. His sense of what the novel could achieve had expanded far beyond Ford's plans for a series of 'workingman' novels, and even beyond Garnett's careful understanding of what could be safely recommended for acceptance by a British publisher. Lawrence's attitude to writing and to ideas is marked by a sense of the newness of what he can do and by a corresponding determination to shake off the conventions and restrictions of the past. It is this mood which comes through strongly in his letter to Garnett.

Garnett had apparently objected to the 'psychology' of the characters in *The Wedding Ring* (*The Rainbow*), and it is to this that Lawrence refers in beginning with the assertion, 'it is only that I have a different attitude to my characters, and that necessitates a different attitude in you, which you are not as yet prepared to give' (*Letters*, II, 182). What Lawrence is trying to avoid, he says, is the 'old-fashioned' way of drawing character, by which the writer would 'conceive a character in a certain moral scheme and make him consistent'. He continues:

The certain moral scheme is what I object to. In Turguenev, and in Tolstoi, and in Dostoievski, the moral scheme into which all the characters fit – and it is nearly the same scheme – is, whatever the extraordinariness of the characters themselves, dull, old, dead. (*Letters*, II, 182–3)

He is not interested, he says, in what a woman in tears 'feels', because 'That presumes an *ego* to feel with'. What the 'ego' makes of itself, observes of itself, is of little interest to him because the ego has narrow preoccupations: it is concerned only with what it can assimilate to itself. He cares, rather, 'about what the woman *is*', by which he means 'what she *is* as a phenomenon (or as representing some greater, inhuman will), instead of what she feels according to the human conception' (*Letters*, II, 183). People, for Lawrence, in other words, are capable of *being* far more – far more potent, far more divine – than is normally perceived, especially if normal perceiving is through the deadness of a 'moral scheme'. Character, therefore, as it is drawn and developed in fiction, should involve a sense of the infinite capacity for *being* that would otherwise pass unnoticed. The Futurists are 'stupid', artistically, because 'Instead of looking for the new human phenomenon, they will only look for the phenomena of the science of physics to be found in human being.' Marinetti is more interested in the molecules of 'a blade of steel' than in 'the laughter or tears of a woman', whereas, says Lawrence, it is what these phenomena have in common that is truly interesting. Lawrence is fascinated by 'the inhuman will', meaning the capacity of the woman to be governed by, to manifest in her being, a force of living that is 'greater' than the human as it is apprehended by other humans.

This all precedes Lawrence's most famous assertion about character.

You mustn't look in my novel for the old stable ego of the character. There is another ego, according to whose action the individual is unrecognisable, and passes through, as it were, allotropic states which it needs a deeper sense than any we've been used to exercise, to discover are states of the same single radically-unchanged element. (Like as diamond and coal are the same pure single element of carbon. The ordinary novel would trace the history of the diamond – but I say 'diamond, what!

This is carbon.' And my diamond might be coal or soot, and my theme is carbon.) (*Letters*, II, 183)

What this adds up to is that characters as portrayed by Lawrence are not necessarily predictable, or understandable, or even consistent, as they were, he believes, in the traditional novel. Mrs Witt's proposal of marriage to the groom Lewes, in *St Mawr*, would be one example of such unpredictability, or Ursula's decision to marry Anton Skrebensky after all at the very end of *The Rainbow*. There is much in the individual that is hidden, not least from him or herself, and while a process in which self-discovery of what has been hidden might or might not take place, nevertheless the driving force of that character will to a large degree be influenced by unrecognised motivations. Hemione's physical assault on Birkin in *Women in Love* is, as we have seen, a powerful incident in which the motivating forces are by no means clear to Hermione herself, and are only made accessible to the reader by the forms of language Lawrence uses to describe her participation in the attack. Yet, as the carbon image expresses, hiddenness and unpredictability do not ultimately mean inconsistency. Or rather, there is a 'deeper' kind of consistency, or 'stability', which underlies the variations (the 'allotropic states') that the basic substance of character goes through. These experiences might not be appreciated by the individual character, or might simply be taken for granted by him or her. But the reader who is prepared to 'exercise' a 'deeper sense' in the reading of Lawrence's fiction will become alert to the 'carbon' that is his theme and to the radical differences, therefore, between a novel by Lawrence and the 'ordinary novel'.

I have stressed already how Lawrence's ideas changed and developed during his writing life, but a quotation from another of his 1925 essays, 'The Novel', suggests that, with regard to character in fiction, the thoughts expressed to Garnett in 1914 did remain as the backbone of his attitude for a significantly long period, a period that included much of his major fiction. Lawrence is discussing *War and Peace*, and compares the character of Tolstoy himself with the character Pierre in the novel. Tolstoy, he says, was 'true to his characters' but 'being a man with a philosophy' (or with a 'certain moral scheme'), he 'wasn't true to his *own character*'. This leads him to a paragraph of general remarks about 'character' in both literature and life.

> Character is a curious thing. It is the flame of a man, which burns brighter or dimmer, bluer or yellower or redder, rising or sinking or flaring according to the draughts of circumstance and the changing air of life, changing itself continually, yet remaining one single, separate flame, flickering in a strange world: unless it be blown out at last by too much adversity. (*Phoenix II*, 423)

As before, the emphasis is on a surface variation and a deeper consistency that does not necessarily explain the variations but rather validates their range and frequency as responses to the events and pressures of 'a strange world'.

The language of character development, then, must not only enable the reader to approach the 'one single, separate flame' of the individual, but show also the range of its variations, bright or dim, blue, yellow or red, as the work of fiction progresses. And understanding of the work will only be possible if sufficient access has been given to what each character 'is'. Yet what this means is that access is sought to that to which the character him or herself probably has very little access, or none at all. What the character, Will Brangwen or Gerald Crich, Baxter Dawes or Mrs Witt, simply goes through, perhaps questioning, perhaps only bewildered, the novelist must make available to his reader in a form that at least holds out the promise of meaning. Language, while not understating the complexity and possibly the tortuousness of the inner lives of characters, must at the same time retain something of its own quality as a way of communicating, of presenting in a logical pattern items of knowledge that would otherwise exist in mute isolation.

In these paragraphs from the 'Anna Victrix' chapter of *The Rainbow*, we see Lawrence straining language to the limits of communicable meaning in order to express the emotions Will Brangwen is in the grip of as he struggles to come to terms with the feelings aroused in him by his new wife Anna.

> For how can a man stand, unless he have something sure under his feet? Can a man tread the unstable water all his life, and call that standing? Better give in and drown at once.

And upon what could he stand, save upon a woman? Was
he then like the old man of the sea, impotent to move save
upon the back of another life? Was he impotent, or a cripple
or a defective, or a fragment? (p. 187)

Almost all the key words here, both nominal and verbal forms
– 'stand', 'feet', 'tread', 'unstable', 'water', 'drown', 'impotent',
'move', 'cripple', 'fragment' – have to be recognised at once as
metaphors if the passage is to make any sense. In particular,
we know that Will is not impotent in the normal sense because
Anna is expecting their first child. Equally, we know he is not
a cripple. The pattern of questions is important in establishing
that here is an individual desperately trying to work out what
it is he is feeling, and so too is Will's reaching out for ever
more unlikely analogies – standing, treading water, drowning,
the old man of the sea, a defective, a fragment – in order to
bring within his mental frame the unaccustomed emotions. At
the same time, though, we remain unsure as readers whether
these words actually express Will's thoughts as they are available
to him, or whether they rather give Lawrence's impression of the
unarticulated sensations that hold him. Will feels like a 'fragment',
incapable of being himself, incapable of holding onto his own
identity. He is uniquely impotent, and the only way out is to
recognise his own separateness and 'drown at once'. For him,
the problem is unprecedented in his experience and he has no
means of relating to it.

But a further dimension to the language of this passage,
and of many others like it in the course of the chapter, is
that in the expression of these feelings Lawrence has bound Will
firmly into the patterns of the novel. He is made to relate, albeit
unconsciously, to the novel's themes of impotence and fulfilment,
and of male-female dependence, as he is to the water of the
Biblical flood, and therefore to the image of the rainbow itself,
and to the actual flood that drowns the first Tom Brangwen.
What is more, the immediate context of the paragraphs, the
chapter itself, provides other patterns both of images and of
linguistic structures, particularly the establishing of the question
as a potent and pressing form of clarifying emotion, and these
patterns gradually enable the reader to recognise and participate
in the language of feeling that Lawrence is developing during this

part of the novel. This is a feature of *The Rainbow* to which we shall return in Chapter 7.

Who is doing the thinking, as we have seen with Will, can be a problem in Lawrence's development of character. He takes for himself the freedom to shift between authorial assertion and thoughts that are unquestionably the character's own, or even the thoughts of more than one character. This can create difficulties for the reader. In this paragraph from *Sons and Lovers*, the opening authorial voice is quickly replaced by thoughts that could be either Miriam's or Paul's.

> They parted. He felt guilty towards her. She was bitter, and she scorned him. He still belonged to herself, she believed; yet he could have Clara, take her home, sit with her next his mother in chapel, give her the same hymn-book he had given herself years before. She heard him running quickly indoors. (p. 396)

We cannot tell for sure whose mind is being taken as the focus for the train of thought and observation that is the subject of this paragraph. 'He felt guilty towards her' suggests that it is Paul, recognising the truth of his own feelings. 'She was bitter, and she scorned him' is therefore Paul's awareness of Miriam's feelings. The next sentence is then initially read as if 'she believed' is Paul's sense of what Miriam was feeling. This reading, however, becomes increasingly hard to maintain as the long fourth sentence continues, and we realise that the weight of detail showing Paul's actions through a series of co-ordinate clauses is actually seen from the outside, from Miriam's point of view. This is finally confirmed by 'herself' in 'given herself years before'. 'She heard him running quickly indoors' can only be Miriam's impression. This gradual consolidation in the reader's mind that the language of this passage is in fact filtered through Miriam's mind means that the early sentences can be reassigned. 'She was bitter, and she scorned him' becomes Miriam recognising the truth of her own feelings. Even 'He felt guilty towards her' is her sense of Paul's feelings based on the immediately preceding conversation. But here a third possibility arises: Paul is the focus for the second sentence, with a switch to Miriam for the third, whereafter Lawrence expands upon her thoughts and observations before returning to expand upon Paul's six lines later ('His heart went hot, and he was angry with them for talking about the girl' (p. 397)). There is no way we can be sure. The language used is distinctive neither to Paul nor to Miriam. The diction is straightforward but the grammatical structure is convoluted. 'He still belonged to herself, she believed' is both inverted and abbreviated: what appears to be the main clause of the sentence, 'He still belonged to herself', in fact turns out to be a subordinate clause once we reach the real main clause, 'she believed'. The false main clause was telling us what she believed in advance of our knowing she believed anything! 'She believed that he still belonged to herself' would be a more conventional way of expressing her thought, though even that would not finally settle whose thought this is.

It is not easy to read writing of this kind. The necessity to reread imposes frustration upon the reader and does not particularly advance the understanding of the character. But in the very ambiguity of the passage above, and in its grammatical tangles, we can also find the clue to its appropriateness as a way of writing for the subject Lawrence is treating here. Paul and Miriam are at this stage still emotionally tied to each other, so much so that it is impossible to distinguish where the emotions of one end and the other's begin. Each is supremely sensitive to the slightest emotional change in the other, which produces a corresponding change in him or herself. What one can tell the other can tell, without knowing whether he or she was responsible for initiating the feeling that led to the recognition of the feeling. The language of this paragraph, and of others like it not only in *Sons and Lovers* but in many later works, especially *The Rainbow* and *Women in Love*, is utilised by Lawrence in the enactment of emotional knots, so that the feelings expressed do not necessarily belong to either one of two people, but rather exist between, are in the process of being played out between, both of them. It is right that the sentences should not with certainty be assignable, initially, to either character, for both characters contribute to the feelings that the language is making accessible to us. And while we are probably no further advanced in understanding precisely what either character '*feels*', we do, perhaps, from our struggles with the language of perplexing emotions, have a better sense of what each of them '*is*' in terms of their 'representing some greater, inhuman will'.

Access to character promises to be much easier for the reader when the narrator can tell in his own voice all we need to know to understand what it is that gives the life to this or that person. This is the traditional novelist's main technique of characterisation. ' My dear little cousin," said he with all the gentleness of an excellent nature, "what can be the matter? ' 'She was open, ardent, and not in the least self-admiring. . . . . ' 'The desire – sober and repressed – of Elizabeth-Jane's heart was indeed to see, to hear, and to understand.'[1] And Lawrence does employ this method. But it is usually reserved for the lesser characters in his fiction, which is certainly not the case with the three examples quoted above, and we frequently find that what we are told is not as revealing as it at first appears to be.

Here, for example, is our introduction to the character Phoenix in *St Mawr*, who appears as a kind of servant to Mrs Witt.

> Out of the debacle of the war she had emerged with an odd piece of debris, in the shape of Gerónimo Trujillo. He was an American, son of a Mexican father and a Navajo Indian mother, from Arizona. When you knew him well, you recognized the real half-breed, though at a glance he might pass as a sunburnt citizen of any nation, particularly of France. He looked like a certain sort of Frenchman, with his curiously-set dark eyes, his straight black hair, his thin black moustache, his rather long cheeks, and his almost slouching, diffident, sardonic bearing. Only when you knew him, and looked right into his eyes, you saw an unforgettable glint of the Indian.
>
> He had been badly shell-shocked, and was for a time a wreck. Mrs Witt, having nursed him into convalescence, asked him where he was going next. He didn't know. His father and mother were dead, and he had nothing to take him back to Phoenix, Arizona. Having had an education in one of the Indian high schools, the unhappy fellow had no place in life at all. Another of the many misfits.
>
> There was something of the Paris *Apache* in his appearance: but he was all the time withheld, and nervously shut inside himself. Mrs Witt was intrigued by him.
>
> 'Very well, Phoenix,' she said, refusing to adopt his Spanish name, 'I'll see what I can do.'
>
> What she did was to get him a place on a sort of manor

farm, with some acquaintances of hers. He was very good with horses, and had a curious success with turkeys and geese and fowls. (pp. 15–16)

The first thing to remark about this introduction is that it is written in a language that owes nothing to the language of the character himself. The closest we come to Phoenix's language is the sentence 'He didn't know', which stands for his having nothing to say for himself. The dominant language of the passage is surprisingly personal, making the pretence that Phoenix is actually a meetable and knowable figure for the reader: 'When you knew him well, you recognized the real half-breed, though at a glance he might pass . . . '; 'Only when you knew him, and looked right into his eyes, you saw an unforgettable glint of the Indian.' The use of the second person pronoun invites participation in the act of knowing the character, as if we could indeed at first 'glance' mistake him for any 'sunburnt citizen', but that we too are capable of 'recognizing the real half-breed', of looking 'right into his eyes' and being impressed by the 'unforgettable glint'. In this context, 'He looked like' is less the novelist's conventional descriptive formula, and more an amplification of the participatory 'glance' that the reader has been invited to give. The long series of nominal groups, each following almost the same pattern ('his straight black hair, his thin black moustache, his rather long cheeks . . . '), conveys the information our first 'glance' would probably take in, and the repeated possessive, 'his', implies that we are learning something real about the man. It is only with the final, longer, group, 'his almost slouching, diffident, sardonic bearing' that a note of caution is sounded as Lawrence breaks the pattern of the nominal groups. The string of modifiers, each one, apparently, not *quite* pinning the character down, suggests the kind of person who would reveal very little of himself to a 'glance', or even to a lengthy scrutiny, and whom it is probably very difficult, and a little dangerous, to 'know well'.

The language of the passage depends for its effectiveness upon a tone that pretends to ease of approach, both between writer and reader and between reader and character and to ease of knowledge. But the real and disturbing effect is achieved through the clashing of this tone with the deeply unknowable quality of Phoenix himself. Nothing that the narrator tells us gives us any

approach at all to the character. The phrases chosen tell only that
he is ungraspable, beyond the conventions of our language. He is
'an odd piece of debris'. He 'was for a time a wreck'. He is an
'unhappy fellow', a 'misfit'. There is 'something' in his appearance
that suggests 'the Paris *Apache*'. We know only what the outside
tells us, and that, as we realise, is deceptive. Everything else
comes to us through his effect on other people: on Mrs Witt,
who is 'intrigued by him'; and on ourselves, increasingly uneasy
in the pretend presence Lawrence is imposing on us, increasingly
unwilling to 'look right into the eyes' of someone who is not
only 'slouching, diffident, sardonic' but 'all the time withheld,
and nervously shut inside himself'.

As we saw with Egbert at the opening of 'England, My England',
Lawrence has set the language of a descriptive passage at odds with
the character who is involved in the description. Here, the choice
of words, the casual tone of addressing the reader, the easy social
assumptions, all fail to come to terms with a figure so remote from
the polite conventions of English writing: Mexican father, Navajo
Indian mother, Spanish name that is never used, shell-shocked,
and known as Phoenix. The 'place on a sort of manor farm, with
some acquaintances of hers' is a crowning irony, for Phoenix is
as out of place in this setting as he is in the English language.
And his 'curious success with turkeys and geese and fowls', with
Lawrence's insistent driving home of the endless domesticity of
the work ('turkeys *and* geese *and* fowls') is a bizarre attempt to
pigeon-hole a man whose nickname suggests unknowably remote
regions of America and the unique legendary bird that is reborn
from its own ashes.

The language of much of *St Mawr* is language that builds
mistrust of itself into its diction and structures. The society
language of the opening shows up its own inadequacies and
the shallowness of the values it incorporates, while the language
that attempts to describe Phoenix betrays its inability to provide
anything more than an unreliable 'glance' at the living truth of
character. But the pattern of the book is one in which layers of
pretence, of unreality, are removed, and while Lou Witt is dra-
matically presented to a 'greater', more 'inhuman' self, Phoenix
finally emerges in a form that can be revealed to the reader in a
language that has the capacity to suggest something of the 'quickness', the vitality of his being. During the course of the story he is

seen riding behind Mrs Witt in Rotten Row, showing his ability
to master St Mawr, and displaying his contempt for Rico. Each
appearance adds something to the 'diffident, sardonic' danger of
his character. Other characters make some attempt to approach
him, and for a moment we see, perhaps, some hint of an insight
into his true being. Lou, for example, discusses Arizona with him.

> He looked at her with a haunted glow in his dark eyes. The
> poor fellow was suffering from nostalgia. And as he glowed at
> her in that queer mystical way, she seemed to see that country,
> with its dark, heavy mountains holding in their lap the great
> stretches of pale, creased, silent desert that still is virgin of
> idea, its word unspoken. (p. 85)

The language here is not the easy social chat of Phoenix's first
appearance, and the impression is that Lou does get closer to him
than has so far been possible. She recognises his home-sickness,
and sees in him something of the mystery of the landscape that
made him. But the language itself is still remote from Phoenix,
from the man who, a paragraph earlier, has given his version of
the landscape: 'And then you see the desert, away below, go miles
and miles, and where the canyon go, the crack where it look red!
I know, I been there, working a cattle ranch.' The language that
can speak of a 'poor fellow' and 'nostalgia' has nothing to say to
a man whose normal expression consists of sentences like 'I been
there, working a cattle ranch'. What Lou sees in Phoenix here
is partly a truth about him – he *is* homesick – and also partly a
truth about herself. She is sick for somewhere she does not yet
recognise. She, too, is 'virgin of idea', yet growing in awareness
that there is an 'idea', a way of being, to which she has not pre-
viously had access but which now is awaiting her. The language
in which her thoughts are transmitted to us, with its rich weight
of modifiers that expand the significance of each nominal group
('haunted', 'dark', 'queer mystical', 'dark, heavy', 'pale, creased,
silent'), is the language of self-conscious articulacy. It is language
on which the thinker can read the meaning of her own thoughts,
and in which the apparent object of the thoughts, Phoenix, is
only one of the items to be expressed. As Lou looks 'right into
his eyes' she sees not the real Phoenix, the 'unforgettable glint
of the Indian', but a picture of what she herself lacks. And that

picture is the more convincing for being expressed in a standard of grammatical English that has little to do with Phoenix and everything to do with Lou's own linguistic background.

The language spoken by Phoenix is marked by verbs that fail to conjugate ('the desert . . . go', 'the canyon . . . go', 'it look red') or that are missing their auxiliaries ('I been there'). It is sparse as the landscape he has been invited to describe, and un-formed as the meaning he attaches to it. He speaks only to give an impression of something that is not available to him in language. What exists in his mind of this landscape is not accessible to him as knowledge: it is simply there, and language can only gesture at its presence. What he says for himself, therefore, is not a truth about himself, as Lou's words are. They do not express him. The only truth they express is the distance between the 'real half-breed' and the capacity of the English language to generate meaningful statements.

But Lawrence does attempt to give a version of the real Phoenix, and when he does so it is back in Arizona when he is restored to at least part of his mixed heritage. What moves Phoenix, we are told, is not the white woman, Lou, who can 'talk clever and know things like a man'. She is not recognised 'as a woman at all'.

In this respect, she didn't exist. It needed the shawled Indian or Mexican women, with their squeaky, plaintive voices, their shuffling, watery humility, and the dark glances of their big, knowing eyes. When an Indian woman looked at him from under her black fringe, with dark, half-secretive suggestion in her big eyes: and when she stood before him hugged in her shawl, in such apparently complete quiescent humility: and when she spoke to him in her mousey squeak of a high, plaintive voice, as if it were difficult for her female bashfulness even to emit so much sound: and when she shuffled away with her legs wide apart, because of her wide-topped, white, high buckskin boots with tiny white feet, and her dark-knotted hair so full of hard, yet subtle lure: and when he remembered the almost watery softness of the Indian woman's dark, warm flesh: then he was a male, an old, secretive, rat-like male. (p. 142)

Even here, of course, there are signs that Lawrence is having to use language that has nothing to do with Phoenix. Phrases like 'quiescent humility', words like 'emit', structures like 'hard, yet subtle lure', are self-consciously English. The passage is the narrator's version of the way Phoenix's thoughts would be expressed if they were expressible. It is an impression of a state of mind rather than a mind actually seen at work. The way the impression is conveyed, however, differs markedly in its linguistic features from the other extracts from *St Mawr* that we have seen. There is a hidden quality about the language used here, arising from the use of structures that do not quite complete themselves, or in which completion is long delayed, or from unexpected mixing of vocabulary. The second sentence, for example, never really resolves itself grammatically: 'It needed the shawled Indian or Mexican women . . . ' to do what? The sentence conveys a measure of insight, but nevertheless fails to reveal the meaning it promises. And in the following very long sentence, the drawn-out patterns of co-ordination and dependence delay the main clause until it is almost forgotten that we are waiting for one. There are five separate adverbial clauses, each beginning 'when', and each of which could singly be resolved by the main clause, 'he was a male'. Within these subordinate clauses, other patterns of subordination set up rival currents of meaning that threaten to lead the sense away from the mainstream of the sentence: 'with dark, half-secretive suggestion in her big eyes'; 'as if it were difficult for her female bashfulness even to emit so much sound'; 'because of her wide-topped, white, high buckskin boots'. Yet the powerful recurrence of 'when' again and again pulls the flow back to its original course, until the sentence finally reaches the almost triumphant 'then he was a male'. Even here, though, at the end of the passage, the unusual mixture in diction which has given a combination like 'shuffling, watery humility', or put 'mousey squeak' before 'shuffled away with her legs wide apart', or contrived the awkward set of modifiers in 'wide-topped, white, high buckskin boots', concludes the sentence with the startling description, 'an old, secretive, rat-like male'. The 'shawled' women have brought about the emergence of the 'secretive' male, and the language in which this has occurred shares something of the 'shawled' or 'secretive' quality. Without being as blatantly non-standard as 'I been there', the structures and diction employed in the passage have carefully missed the normal grammatical logic of English writing.

In doing so, of course, Lawrence's writing has managed to give a more complete insight into the character in *St Mawr* who has least relation to the structures of English. When we read this passage, so close to the end of the story, we realise how wide of the mark the first description of Phoenix was, with its 'sunburnt citizen of any nation'. The gulf between the 'rat-like male' and the associations of the term 'citizen', or even of 'sunburnt', is immense. Nor does Lou's 'nostalgia', or her recognition of the 'queer mystical way' that he 'glowed', come close to the man who is only in touch with himself when he can read the 'dark, half-secretive suggestion' in the 'big eyes' of an Indian woman. It is to Lou's credit, the white woman who for Phoenix does not 'exist' as a woman at all, that by this stage in the book she is sensitive to what has until now been silent in his character. And if Lawrence wishes us to endorse Lou's criticism of this truth of Phoenix's being, that his opinion of his own maleness is 'childish' and 'stupid', with its 'furtive lurking in holes and imagining it could not be detected' (p. 143), nevertheless she also seems to speak for the author when she concludes that 'one half of his intelligence was a complete dark blank' and finds 'a relief' in the unknowable quality this retains for him (p. 144).

Access to character, then, can be afforded through a variety of techniques, each of which has implications for language use. Even, in the case of Phoenix, when much that is given is quickly or gradually revealed as mistaken, or inadequate, it is still a kind of truth that such mistakes can be made. What access to character frequently involves, we realise, is the limitations on perception imposed by the various agents of access. The language adopted to permit access will share the values and shortcomings of the society or character from which or from whom the language derives. When Lou looks at Phoenix, or at anyone else, she sees through her own limitations. What those limitations are depends on the stage she has reached in her development over the course of the story. And if her perceptions of Phoenix contribute to our capacity to read the 'carbon' of his character, they have an even more significant role to play in enabling us to perceive the 'allotropic states' through which she is passing and thereby to begin to understand 'what she *is*'.

The opening chapter of *Women in Love* is a striking example in Lawrence's fiction of several kinds of access to character working in succession, or rather of access to five main characters: Ursula and Gudrun Brangwen, Hermione Roddice, Gerald

Crich and Rupert Birkin. Dialogue, action, external and internal description, and internal monologue are all used, with the effect not only of introducing five separate people, five self-contained and independent existences, but of showing something of their mutual dependence, their existences within each others' minds and emotions. And again, what can be conveyed depends upon the linguistic resources that are legitimately available to Lawrence.

First of all, in a rather low-key opening, Ursula and Gudrun are at home in 'their father's house in Beldover, working and talking'. Lawrence tells us that 'They were mostly silent, talking as their thoughts strayed through their minds.'

'Ursula,' said Gudrun, 'don't you *really* want to get married?' Ursula laid her embroidery in her lap and looked up. Her face was calm and considerate.

'I don't know,' she replied. 'It depends how you mean.'

Gudrun was slightly taken aback. She watched her sister for some moments.

'Well,' she said, ironically, 'it usually means one thing! But don't you think, anyhow, you'd be – ' she darkened slightly – 'in a better position than you are in now.'

A shadow came over Ursula's face.

'I might,' she said. 'But I'm not sure.'

Again, Gudrun paused, slightly irritated. She wanted to be quite definite.

'You don't think one needs the *experience* of having been married?' she asked.

'Do you think it need *be* an experience?' replied Ursula.

'Bound to be, in some way or other,' said Gudrun, coolly. 'Possibly undesirable, but bound to be an experience of some sort.'

'Not really,' said Ursula. 'More likely to be the end of experience.'

Gudrun sat very still, to attend to this.

'Of course,' she said, 'there's *that* to consider.' This brought the conversation to a close. Gudrun, almost angrily, took up her rubber and began to rub out part of her drawing. Ursula stitched absorbedly. (p. 7)

Two features are immediately apparent here. The first is that very little is actually communicated between the two sisters through their dialogue, which is sparse and consists largely of expressions like 'I don't know', 'anyhow' and 'in some way or other'. Their language, of course, places them in the social scale, as does their activity, embroidery and drawing, but it also, by its very sparseness, indicates that the communication that is taking place between them arises not just from the words they speak. The mood of the passage is one of gently rising irritation, and while the evasiveness of both questions and answers is partly responsible for this, the narrative setting for the conversation has a much larger part to play. The second feature, then, is that Lawrence cannot rely solely on the words his characters speak, which is what he would have to do if he were writing a play. There is authorial commentary, and it is this that gives the mood of irritation to a conversation that could, with a different commentary, be light-hearted and jokey without any change in wording. Most of the tone of the conversation is conveyed through commentary – 'she darkened slightly', the 'shadow' on Ursula's face – and often through a single adverb – 'ironically', 'coolly'. The use of italics is an authorial indication of *how* the words are spoken. And commentary is used to describe both the deeper effects made by the conversation on the characters and something of their motivations: 'Her face was calm and considerate'; 'Gudrun was slightly taken aback'; 'She wanted to be quite definite'; 'almost angrily . . . absorbedly'.

What we see in this extract are the limitations of dialogue for giving access to character and motivation. The sisters discuss marriage and experience, which are to be central preoccupations of the book. But there is insufficient scope in what is expected to be a reasonably life-like conversation for the kind of introduction to character that is necessary on the first page of a novel. For this reason, Lawrence is obliged to amplify the dialogue through the voice of the narrator, in order to have said what neither Ursula nor Gudrun is able realistically to say for herself.

But the overall impression of the scene is, in fact, one that does add considerably to the reader's awareness of characters and of their inter-relatedness. The growing irritation within the scene arises from each sister's alertness to the mood of the other: they are mutually sensitive to the unspoken features of the conversation of which the reader needs to be told. The pauses, the shadows, the tones of irony or coolness, are all made explicit to the reader, but at the same time the reader is aware that these features are registered within the minds of the two participants without the necessity for any statement whatsoever. We are not told 'Gudrun saw a shadow come over Ursula's face', or 'Ursula saw that Gudrun was irritated', and the fact that we are not is itself significant because it means that we can take it for granted. What the language tells us is what needs to be communicated to us as readers. What is communicated between the sisters is not confined to the realm of language. There emerges, in other words, a relationship between two people that exists independently of the words that happen to be spoken on this particular occasion, and which, like other relationships, is a complex network of mutual sensitivities and shared knowledge of each other over a long period.

As the chapter progresses, Lawrence takes his characters out of their home and walks them through Beldover to see the wedding of one of the Crich daughters. As they stand outside the church, watching the carriages arrive, we are given the impression made by each guest on the mind of Gudrun. Most significantly, she watches the arrival of Mrs Crich and her son Gerald.

> Her son was of a fair, sun-tanned type, rather above middle height, well-made, and almost exaggeratedly well-dressed. But about him also was the strange, guarded look, the unconscious glisten, as if he did not belong to the same creation as the people about him. Gudrun lighted on him at once. There was something northern about him that magnetized her. In his clear northern flesh and his fair hair was a glisten like sunshine refracted through crystals of ice. And he looked so new, unbroached, pure as an arctic thing. Perhaps he was thirty years old, perhaps more. His gleaming beauty, maleness, like a young, good-humoured, smiling wolf, did not blind her to the significant, sinister stillness in his bearing, the lurking danger of his unsubdued temper. 'His totem is the wolf,' she repeated to herself. 'His mother is an old, unbroken wolf.' And then she experienced a keen paroxysm, a transport, as if she had made some incredible discovery, known to nobody else on earth. (pp. 15–16)

We find here the 'slightly modified repetition' that is characteristic of Lawrence's writing when he is dealing with emotional excitement. Not only are single words and phrases repeated – 'northern', 'glisten', 'wolf' – but, less obtrusively, grammatical structures within sentences. The nominal group 'the strange, guarded look' is immediately followed by a co-ordinate group, 'the unconscious glisten'. Similarly, 'his clear northern flesh' is followed by 'his fair hair', 'new' by 'unbroached', 'the significant, sinister stillness in his bearing' by 'the lurking danger of his unsubdued temper', and 'a keen paroxysm' by 'a transport'. At times, it seems that Lawrence is simply scattering his writing with synonyms – 'glisten', 'lighted', 'sunshine', 'gleaming'; or 'sinister stillness', 'lurking danger' – or with self-consciously clever patterns, like the 'something northern' that 'magnetized her'. Certainly, in view of Gerald's death in the snows of the Swiss Alps at the end of the novel, the insistence here at his first appearance on the 'northern', the 'arctic' and the 'crystals of ice' in his appearance does seem rather ponderously significant. But one of the positive achievements of the passage is that a real sense of impact is made by one of the major characters of the novel, and made not by Lawrence's simply telling us about him, but through the perception and response of a character with whom we have already become familiar.

The structure of the passage is such that we are moved from the more detached observation of the opening sentence towards the 'paroxysm' and beyond to even more breathless reactions by Gudrun. Even the opening is marked by a mixture of the factual, 'fair, sun-tanned . . . above middle height', and the value judgement, 'well-made, and almost exaggeratedly well-dressed', that reminds us that the eyes through which we are seeing are Gudrun's and that we must therefore expect her assessment of what she sees as well as factual observation. The second sentence is more impressionistic. The language is less accessible, and it is up to the reader to decide what Gudrun might mean by 'the unconscious glisten' (or, more strictly, what Lawrence might mean on Gudrun's behalf) or by the phrases that follow as her response becomes more and more heightened. The low key of the first pages of the novel has been replaced by a new emotional level, and to achieve this Lawrence has changed his narrative tactics. There is no longer commentary, a medium for communication between narrator and reader. The narrative voice has surrendered to the force of one character, and the language embodies in its range and structures the immediacy of that character's response as well as prefiguring, as a kind of instinctive foreknowledge on Gudrun's part, the course of her relationship with Gerald during the rest of the novel: danger, isolation, pain and death. Lawrence has opened up a different narrative realm, and it is one in which fewer concessions are made to the reader. The priority is to give the impression of character through a focus on unusually heightened emotion, when the individual is less her everyday self, and yet is more in touch with a deeper, unrecognised self. As Gudrun exclaims a moment later, 'Good God! . . . what is this?' And what this is, irrespective of the unease with which we might respond to Lawrence's linguistic strategies, is what she '*is*'.

As if to underline the emotional peculiarity of Gudrun's response to Gerald, Lawrence immediately shifts his focus in the following paragraph to the more normal level of Ursula's mind. 'The bridesmaids were here, and yet the bridegroom had not come. Ursula wondered if something was amiss, and if the wedding would yet go all wrong.' (p. 16) Hermione arrives, and as Ursula watches her we are told what Ursula knows about her: 'She was passionately interested in reform, her soul was given up to the public cause. But she was a man's woman, it was the manly world that held her.' (p. 17) But in a remarkably daring narrative switch, Lawrence suddenly leaves Ursula's perceptions and we find that we are experiencing Hermione's personality as Hermione herself experiences it.

> And yet her soul was tortured, exposed. Even walking up the path to the church, confident as she was that in every respect she stood beyond all vulgar judgement, knowing perfectly that her appearance was complete and perfect, according to the first standards, yet she suffered a torture, under her confidence and her pride, feeling herself exposed to wounds and to mockery and to despite. She always felt vulnerable, vulnerable, there was always a secret chink in her armour. She did not know herself what it was. It was a lack of robust self, she had no natural sufficiency, there was a terrible void, a lack, a deficiency of being within her. (pp. 17–18)

And from within Hermione's mind we have, in the very next paragraph, our introduction to the character of Birkin.

And she wanted someone to close up this deficiency, to close it up for ever. She craved for Rupert Birkin. When he was there, she felt complete, she was sufficient, whole. For the rest of time she was established on the sand, built over a chasm, and, in spite of all her vanity and securities, any common maid-servant of positive, robust temper could fling her down this bottomless pit of insufficiency, by the slightest movement of jeering or contempt. . . .

He was perverse too. He fought her off, he always fought her off. The more she strove to bring him to her, the more he battled her back. And they had been lovers now, for years. Oh, it was so wearying, so aching; she was so tired. But still she believed in herself. (p. 18)

Again there is repetition and a high proportion of co-ordination in sentence structure. She was 'tortured, exposed'; she knows 'perfectly' that her appearance is 'complete and perfect'; she feels 'exposed to wounds and to mockery and to despite'. But while the repetition during Gudrun's reaction to Gerald gives a sense of excited emotion seeking some manner of expression, here its function is different. There is still heightened emotion, but Hermione's feelings are not suddenly visited upon her: they are with her all the time. The repetition, therefore, is that of a mental effort that must be perpetually renewed in order to conceal the 'secret chink in her armour'. While the outside, with which Ursula has already been impressed, is kept 'perfectly', 'complete and perfect', by a deliberate act of will, her inner awareness returns again and again to her own 'exposure' where she is 'vulnerable, vulnerable'. She is possessed by her vulnerability, so that between her consciousness of that and her need to keep up appearances, there is no leisure for language to operate with any flexibility. She has not the mental space for any linguistic creativity, which is what we find in Gudrun's response to Gerald. Hermione is confined by the repetitiveness of the language that defines what she '*is*', rather than reaching out for it in order to assimilate new experience.

This is most noticeable in the final sentence of the first passage, which is in fact three sentences jumbled into one, the last of which threatens to overrun its bounds. With 'there was a terrible void, a lack, a deficiency of being within her', we feel the very edge of Hermione's self-control. The sentence within a sentence is the third of three co-ordinating main clauses, and therefore the 'modified' repetition of something we have been told twice already. It also sprawls across three final fruitless attempts to pin down what is wrong with her: 'a terrible void', 'a lack', 'a deficiency', the second of which simply repeats the 'lack' of the first clause of the whole sentence. The language that has been at least attempting to hold together the deficiency in Hermione finds the 'void' beginning to threaten its very structure.

It is significant that our introduction to Birkin is in terms of his necessity to 'close up' a 'deficiency'. He is experienced through the language of the 'void' and is introduced to provide some firmness to the linguistic structures of the writing: 'She craved for Rupert Birkin.' The simplicity of this sentence after the increasingly formless repetitive nature of those that have preceded it suggests the simplicity, from Hermione's point of view, of the solution to her problems. She is made complete by Birkin. Yet the language that begins to develop the sense of her completeness is itself marked by the same repetition that is characteristic of her deficiency. 'When he was there, she felt complete, she was sufficient, whole.' Again, we find the parallel main clauses, the second of which has tacked onto it a second attempt at describing sufficiency. Her completeness cannot find easy expression, cannot exist within itself, but needs to annexe more and more linguistic items as if seeking security in its own restating. The reason for this, of course, is that Hermione is far from secure in Birkin's love.

In fact the language that describes Birkin's response is more sure of itself than that which, fleetingly, attempts to picture Hermione's completeness. The repetition in 'He fought her off, he always fought her off' is of quite a different order again. It is an unashamed, remorseless repetition of exactly the same words, giving a sentence of two identical main clauses, apart from the significant addition of the adverb 'always', which states what the pattern of the two clauses has already expressed. And the next sentence exactly enacts the state of the relationship between them: 'The more she strove to bring him to her, the more he battled her back.' The operation of Hermione, the subject of the first clause, upon Birkin, its complement, is matched by and produces a corresponding operation by the subject of the second clause, Birkin, upon its complement, Hermione. They are locked against each other, emotionally and grammatically, and as one changes position within the sentence structure, the other makes a change which maintains their opposing functions. In contrast, we can look ahead to the sentences that describe the satisfaction of Birkin and Ursula after love-making: 'She had her desire fulfilled. He had his desire fulfilled.' (p. 360) Identical sentence structures enact mutual fulfilment, with the distinction in personal pronouns marking the only difference within a fully shared experience. Hermione, having been lovers with Birkin 'for years', is forced by that thought into an exclamation of lonely self-awareness: 'Oh, it was so wearying . . . ' And again the repetition, 'so . . . ', expresses the endless attempt to pin down her acknowledged lack of completeness. These are the pressures that culminate in Chapter 8 of the novel in Hermione's physical assault on Birkin.

By an unusual set of shifts in narrative focus, then, Lawrence has allowed the reader access to the five leading characters in his novel, and done so in a way that mixes the existence they acknowledge to themselves with the existence they have for other people. Gerald and Birkin are known at this stage only through the impressions they make on others: their exposure to the reader in their own right follows the importance we know they have already acquired in the emotional lives of Gudrun and Hermione. Ursula is used for much of the chapter as a centre of stability to which Lawrence returns after the linguistic disturbances of the other two women. In this way he is able to maintain a rhythm both in the emotions he is dealing with and in the language that expresses them. The emotional balance for the moment is between Gudrun and Hermione, although in due course Hermione will be superseded by Ursula. None of the characters, however, is allowed to be known simply in isolation: on the contrary, the access we are afforded to each character is through the filter of a major relationship, either the 'subsidiary' one of sister to sister, or the 'great relationship' of man and woman. If Gerald is present in the scene but unconscious of his effect on Gudrun, and if Birkin is absent at this stage but no doubt conscious of Hermione's obsession with him, it is still the case that the reader's initial access to their characters is through their part in a relationship, either potential or actual. And the linguistic tactics Lawrence has used have ensured that as we begin to learn what the characters feel we also gain in understanding of what they are.

The language of the opening of *Women in Love* is language that belongs to the characters themselves and that deals with sensations and emotions that they themselves acknowledge. They are, at this stage in the novel, linguistically responsible adults. They are from an affluent and educated middle or, in Hermione's case, upper class. Elsewhere in the range of Lawrence's fictional writing we find characters who are far less capable of taking the responsibility for their own language, either because of their limited linguistic competence (Phoenix) or because they lack for a while the capacity to come to terms with their own pressing emotional needs (Paul and Miriam, Will Brangwen). This chapter has been able to consider only a few of the linguistic tactics Lawrence uses to give access to character, to relationships and to the 'states' through which characters and relationships can pass. Language, by its very nature, tends to 'put a stamp' on what it deals with. It is a system in its own right, with rules and a logic of its own which will not necessarily do justice to the hidden logic of inner motivation or the emotional logic of human relationships. In 'tracing the history of the diamond' the 'ordinary' novelist shows himself bound by a traditional conception of character and, therefore, by a traditional understanding of the possibilities of language in character portrayal. But to write about 'carbon' calls for flexibility and inventiveness, for 'another language almost' (*Letters*, II, 132). Above all, the novelist must avoid being subject to the 'scheme' that is conventional language, if he is to do justice to the 'great relationships' of our lives, and if his novel is to fulfil its ultimate purpose of being a 'moral' work.

If a novel reveals true and vivid relationships, it is a moral work, no matter what the relationship may consist in. If the novelist *honours* the relationship in itself, it will be a great novel. (*Phoenix*, p. 530)

7   *The Rainbow*

One of the major patterns to emerge from a reading of
The Rainbow is that of the shifting relationship between what
Lawrence calls 'the heated, blind intercourse of farm-life' and
'the spoken world beyond' (p. 8), and this fact alone is enough to
make the novel one of the most interesting and challenging of his
entire achievement in fiction. During the course of this chapter I
shall be discussing some of the most significant manifestations and
expressions of this pattern, both in terms of the way Lawrence
manipulates and exploits the resources of language and in terms
of the engagement with the subject of language itself as a primary
preoccupation of the novel. *The Rainbow* is itself about language,
about the relations that are possible between articulacy and
inarticulacy, between expression and the inexpressible, between
speech and silence, and is therefore peculiarly appropriate for
special treatment in a discussion of Lawrence's language.

The outlines of the pattern are drawn in over the first section
of Chapter 1 of the novel. If the security of 'the heated, blind
intercourse' is evident in the strongly metaphoric language and
flowing rhythms of the opening pages, the encroachment of 'the
spoken world' is also read as early as the seventh paragraph, in
which the women 'were aware of the lips and the mind of the
world speaking and giving utterance, they heard the sound in
the distance, and they strained to listen' (p. 8). For the men,
nature, the 'farm-life', needs no articulating. It is simply taken
as given, just as the landscape and its tone is taken as given:
'The Brangwens had lived for generations on the Marsh Farm,
in the meadows where the Erewash twisted sluggishly through
alder trees, separating Derbyshire from Nottinghamshire.' (p. 7)
The movement of the tenses and verbal forms (past perfect – 'had
lived'; simple past – 'twisted'; present participle – 'separating') is

the assured unselfconscious movement of passing time: what had been, what was, what is continuing. The continuity of the cycles of farm existence is reflected in the continuity of the Brangwens, each generation indistinguishable from the last, and each individual assimilated into the established pattern of the breed: their looks and manners – 'fresh, blond, slow-speaking people'; their assumptions – 'There was a look in the eyes of the Brangwens as if they were expecting something unknown, about which they were eager'; their race memory – 'they had forgotten what it was to be in straitened circumstances'; even the pronoun that can embrace all Brangwens within the repeated third person 'they' (p. 7). The inertness of their brains and the heavy flow of their blood (p. 8) reflect the identity and movement of the Erewash that so gives its tone to the landscape that it achieves nothing more active than to separate Derbyshire from Nottinghamshire. Nor do the 'alder trees' require the definite article to assert their identity: they just are.

Here is nature needing no justification to the men who live by it: its ways are their ways, and the relationship is expressed in a language that is itself bold and lacking in subtlety, and which makes no concessions to character or individuality, because character and individuality at this stage in the novel are necessarily lacking. Men and women and the relations between them require, as discussed in Chapter 6, distinctive and subtly differentiated language if they are to be duly honoured. The opening of *The Rainbow* honours not men and women but a life that is virtually unconscious, and virtually pre-linguistic. We are reading of movements that require no human consciousness, and the consciousness that there is can be given in the vaguest of terms: 'he was aware of something standing above him and beyond him in the distance' (p. 7). So, Lawrence provides us with sentence structures that rely heavily on co-ordination in order to build up the sense of a slow but relentless force gradually moving through the phases of its fulfilment: 'They knew the intercourse between heaven and earth, sunshine drawn into the breast and bowels, the rain sucked up in the daytime, nakedness that comes under the wind in autumn, showing the birds' nests no longer worth hiding.' (p. 8). Here what is 'known' is the headword 'intercourse'. But the co-ordinating clauses, 'sunshine . . . bowels', 'the rain . . . day-time' and 'nakedness . . . autumn' are also 'known' in that they amplify and work out the metaphorical assertion 'the intercourse between heaven and earth'. Each item could be 'known' in its own right, but together they constitute a cycle and a pattern of seasonal and linguistic variety (the presence or absence of the definite article, the passive 'drawn into' and 'sucked up' as against the active 'comes') within the dominant relation of co-ordination. The final clause, 'showing the birds' nests no longer worth hiding', presents an extraordinary shift of scale after the 'intercourse' and the 'sucking up' of the rain, and does so in a shift of syntactical relation, for 'showing . . . ' is a subordinate adjectival clause depending on 'nakedness'. This shift is significant, for it enables Lawrence to achieve both a contrast in the kinds of knowledge that co-exist within the Brangwen mind and a sense of the clumsiness that such pre-linguistic knowledge involves. If the strikingly visual detail of the exposed nests gives a sudden clarity to the sentence, it also emphasises the everyday reality of knowing 'the intercourse between heaven and earth'. The poetic phrases and the swelling rhythms ('the pulse of the blood of the teats of the cows beat into the pulse of the hands of the men' (p. 8)) are all above and beyond the mental grip of the Brangwens themselves: the honour and the identity are Nature's, and the language expresses the rhythms and unconcern of Nature. What the men see, what this knowledge comes down to, is empty birds' nests.

Seen alongside his kind, Tom Brangwen, the first Brangwen to approach the distinctiveness of character, represents a considerable advance towards the 'spoken world beyond'. No preceding Brangwen, after all, is given anything to say, though we are told of Alfred's 'teasing tone' (p. 13) and the younger Alfred's 'broad Derbyshire accent' (p. 14). And even Tom is not permitted to speak for himself until some eight pages of narration have brought him up to early manhood. The dialogue, appropriately, is with a girl:

'When must you get back?' she asked.
'I'm not particular,' he said.
There the conversation again broke down.
Brangwen's companions were ready to go on.
'Art commin', Tom,' they called, 'or art for stoppin'?'

'Ay, I'm commin',' he replied, rising reluctantly, an angry sense of futility and disappointment spreading over him. (p. 22)

Lawrence toys with Tom's inarticulacy, his unfamiliarity with the spoken word, and the contrast between 'Ay, I'm commin'' and the language of his 'angry sense of futility and disappointment' is inevitable.

The same show of inarticulacy is made when Tom speaks at Anna's wedding. Here, too, Lawrence is toying. The narrative preliminaries to Tom's speech are self-consciously articulate:

> The marriage party went across the graveyard to the wall, mounted it by the little steps, and descended. Oh a vain white peacock of a bride perching herself on the top of the wall and giving her hand to the bridegroom on the other side, to be helped down! The vanity of her white, slim, daintily-stepping feet, and her arched neck. (p. 136)

The first sentence here is relatively straightforward, with three main clauses describing the successive stages of the route to the cottage, though in a novel for which the ceremonies and sacraments of the church are as important as the cycle of the seasons we should not miss the pointed irony of having the wedding party cross the graveyard in order to reach home. But the second and third sentences, in which Lawrence rhapsodises over Anna, display a delight in the manipulation of words that is far beyond the appreciation of Tom who is shortly to attempt to speak. There is the opening exclamation, indicating a change of tone from the preceding sentence and a shift in narrative stance from detachment to amused celebration. There is the use of present participles ('perching' and 'giving') as the verbal forms, thus giving to the sentence a structural equivalent to the poise of Anna balanced on top of the wall, waiting for the firm resolution of being 'helped down'. There are the modifiers accumulating, repeating and forming themselves into compounds ('vain white', 'white, slim, daintily-stepping'). There is even the sly allusion to Lawrence's first novel in 'a vain white peacock'. This is the style into which Tom is to fit: 'Tom Brangwen wanted to make a speech. For the first time in his life, he must spread himself wordily.' (p. 137)

Even when Tom is allowed to begin, Lawrence constantly frustrates his attempts to 'spread himself wordily', for he has him interrupted by the rest of the company in a manner that mocks both what he is trying to say and his capacity to say it.

'Marriage,' he began, his eyes twinkling and yet quite profound, for he was deeply serious and hugely amused at the same time, 'Marriage,' he said, speaking in the slow, full-mouthed way of the Brangwens, 'is what we're made for – '

'Let him talk,' said Alfred Brangwen, slowly and inscrutably, 'let him talk.' . . .

'There's no marriage in heaven,' went on Tom Brangwen; 'but on earth there is marriage.'

'That's the difference between 'em,' said Alfred Brangwen, mocking.

'Alfred,' said Tom Brangwen, 'keep your remarks till afterwards, and then we'll thank you for them. – There's very little else, on earth, but marriage. You can talk about making money, or saving souls. You can save your own soul seven times over, and you may have a mint of money, but your soul goes gnawin', gnawin', gnawin', and it says there's something it must have. In heaven there is no marriage. But on earth there *is* marriage, else heaven drops out, and there's no bottom to it.'

'Just hark you now,' said Frank's wife.

'Go on, Thomas,' said Alfred sardonically.

'*If* we've got to be Angels,' went on Tom Brangwen, haranguing the company at large, 'and if there is no such thing as a man nor a woman amongst them, then it seems to me as married couples makes one Angel.'

'It's the brandy,' said Alfred Brangwen wearily. (pp. 137–8)

The realisation that Lawrence is deliberately making things difficult for Tom should not blind us to the fact that he is also making him address two of the leading topics of the novel. In addressing the wedding company on the subject of marriage, Tom is giving a view of the 'great relationship', 'the relation between man and woman'. In presenting this relationship in terms of a contrast with the affairs of the world and the behaviour of individuals ('making money, or saving souls') he is also giving a brief but pointed summary both of the history of the Brangwens and of his own spiritual salvation. The early Brangwens 'had forgotten what it was to be in straitened circumstances', they had no want of money (p. 7), their monetary transactions and advances are carefully chronicled (they 'received a fair sum of money' for the canal across their land (p. 12)) as 'they became richer' (p. 12). But the early Brangwens also looked up from the fields and 'saw the church-tower at Ilkeston in the empty sky'. The Brangwen man 'was aware of something standing above him and beyond him in the distance' (p. 7). Making 'a mint of money' goes with the soul that is 'gnawin', gnawin', gnawin' ', aware of 'something' above and beyond, knowing 'there's something it must have', but prevented by inarticulacy from clarifying what the 'something' is. Thus, the men remain inert while the women look out 'to the spoken world beyond'.

The fact that Tom is actually speaking of these things, using expressions like 'You can talk about making money, or saving souls', is a measure of his advance from the pre-linguistic to the linguistic state. Lawrence's making this a formal speech delivered to a company that cannot resist answering back underlines the point that the Brangwens are engaging in 'the spoken world', albeit in a rudimentary way. Tom's description of the 'gnawin' ' of the soul is a version, no less compelling for being rudimentary, of the kind of spiritual experience that early in the novel has had to be communicated by the narrator on Tom's behalf:

> But during the long February nights with the ewes in labour, looking out from the shelter into the flashing stars, he knew he did not belong to himself. He must admit that he was only fragmentary, something incomplete and subject. There were the stars in the dark heaven travelling, the whole host passing by on some eternal voyage. So he sat small and submissive to the greater ordering. (p. 40)

Again, we see a character sensing his own incompleteness in terms of something above and beyond, and again the articulacy that expresses that sense does not derive from the character himself. The narrative act allows us to read and understand something that for the character is not to do with words. When Tom does make the endeavour to enter 'the spoken world', not only are his words given force by the lived experience that has already been communicated on his behalf. We realise, too, that both narrator and character are engaged in a linguistic encounter in which different forms of language, ranging from the lyrical assurance of the narrative to the compulsive repetition of a single word, 'gnawin', gnawin', gnawin' ', struggle to give expression to one of the most fundamental aspects of being human. There is a truth about the spiritual life to be told, but language can only come close to telling it by adopting various modes, by being heard through the medium of various voices: the narrator's, Tom's, and, at different times, Lydia's, Anna's, Will's, Ursula's. No single voice is capable of speaking the whole truth alone. What is more, the very fact that Lawrence draws attention to this incapacity is a comment about the shortcomings of the enterprise in which he is engaged – writing a novel, using language for the purpose of artistic communication. This is one way in which language, its potential and its limitations, is a subject that is actively engaged with in the writing and reading of *The Rainbow*.

When Tom makes his 'angel' speech, he has, of course, passed on from the smallness and incompleteness of 'the long February nights' to the relative fulfilment of his marriage with Lydia, and this, too, is a lived experience that gives force to his wish to celebrate 'the great relationship' at Anna's wedding. Here, too, the forms of expression Tom adopts fit into larger patterns of the novel's treatment of love and spiritual well-being. The 'empty sky' of the early Brangwens has become for Tom 'the span of the heavens' in which he has found his meeting-place with Lydia in married love (p. 97). His talk of heaven as opposed to earth, therefore, and of a married couple making 'one Angel', marks the contrast between Tom's progress away from his own spiritual isolation and the pattern of spiritual separateness between Brangwen men and Brangwen women, generation after generation.

Even the fact of Tom's relative inarticulacy that is so ruthlessly shown up by the ease and assurance of the narrative has a place in the pattern of the novel. In one perspective, the narrative is a model of 'the spoken world beyond', for not only is its existence entirely dependent on language, but it is wholly above and beyond the lives of the characters. To the extent that it is above and beyond it is also separate, occupying a place apart from the lived experience of the characters. This is the traditional dimension of the third person narrator, and accounts for the shock of reading, as we do later in the novel, Lawrence's harangue of Skrebensky, filled as it is with personal anger and outrage at a character from whom we expect the narrator to remain relatively detached. If the linguistic capacities of the characters can rarely render a just account of their inner lives either to the reader or to themselves, and therefore are required to rely on the narrative voice that proceeds over and above them, the articulacy of the narrator also has limitations. What the narrator lacks is, inevitably, the lived experience that can make language fully human.

We have seen the language of the narrative successfully enacting the emotions and experiences of characters, both in *The Rainbow* and in other novels – Hermione in *Women in Love*, for example – but it does so most successfully when the character dealt with is himself relatively articulate. When approaching less articulate characters – Phoenix in *St Mawr* – Lawrence has to find a way of making the denial of access part of the treatment of character: Phoenix is largely unknowable because he is in an alien society and is seen through the eyes of the likes of Lou and Mrs Witt. This limitation in narrative articulacy is made particularly apparent at moments of emotional fullness. Tom's angel speech is more genuine because of its limitations in articulacy than the narrator's self-conscious cleverness in relishing the spectacle of Anna in her finery. Where the 'heated intercourse' gains over 'the spoken world beyond' is in its emotional engagement. The characters on whom Lawrence focuses in *The Rainbow* have largely moved at least some way from the unselfconscious blindness of the early Brangwens, and are able to attempt an expression of their feelings, yet those feelings are still overwhelmingly real for them. There is not the distance between self and feeling that makes for self-conscious expression. What this means is that the expression we have virtually *is* the feeling. It is not an account of the feeling, which is what the third person narrator would risk making of it. This is a distinction Lawrence makes when writing about a poem by Ralph Hodgson, 'The Song of Honour': 'The feeling is there, right enough – but not in itself, only represented' (*Letters*, II, 92).

One of the most significant moments in Tom's emotional life comes when he first sees Lydia Lensky.

Slowly turning the curve at the steepest part of the slope, his horse britching between the shafts, he saw a woman approaching. But he was thinking for the moment of the horse.

Then he turned to look at her. She was dressed in black, was apparently rather small and slight, beneath her long black cloak, and she wore a black bonnet. She walked hastily, as if unseeing, her head rather forward. It was her curious, absorbed, flitting motion, as if she were passing unseen by everybody, that first arrested him.

She had heard the cart, and looked up. Her face was pale and clear, she had thick dark eyebrows and a wide mouth, curiously held. He saw her face clearly, as if by a light in the air. He saw her face so distinctly, that he ceased to coil on himself, and was suspended.

'That's her,' he said involuntarily. As the cart passed by, splashing through the thin mud, she stood back against the bank. Then, as he walked still beside his britching horse, his eyes met hers. He looked quickly away, pressing back his head, a pain of joy running through him. He could not bear to think of anything. (p. 29)

The language that leads up to Tom's involuntary expression draws attention to itself only in one or two instances. The word 'britching', for example, is Nottinghamshire dialect, meaning 'taking the strain', as a horse does against a load when descending a slope.[1] And yet the attention that is drawn is completely within the frame of Tom's linguistic competence, as if the narrator is relinquishing the hold that conventional articulacy must inevitably exert on the language of the narrative in order to prepare for Tom's realisation. There is also a distinctive grouping of modifiers – 'curious, absorbed, flitting' – to the headword 'motion', distinctive in that three adjectives are used to highlight the fact that the woman's movement is intended to be 'unseen'. While this is indeed a distinctive feature of Lydia's state of mind at this period, as we subsequently discover, it is also significant that Tom's attention is initially 'arrested' by her apparent desire to remain as if absent. She is thus presented as the embodiment of the emptiness that is Tom's inheritance as a Brangwen: he is at first thinking of something else, she is hidden beneath her black clothes (indeed, the enveloping 'black' changes its form from noun to repeated adjective as the sentence describes her appearance), he first notices her 'unseen' quality, and only then is able to see 'her face clearly'.

It is Tom's 'That's her' that succinctly captures the emotional impact of the encounter. Measured against Tom's own capacity for clarity of expression earlier in the novel – the conversation with the foreigner, that so excites Tom, is entirely narrated, apart from two direct remarks by the foreigner – 'That's her' is the first occasion on which he, or anyone else, is able to respond adequately to emotion through language. It is a statement that represents a rare coming together of the 'heated intercourse' and 'the spoken world'. Tom 'involuntarily' uses language that expresses emotion at the same time that it is the emotion. If the marriage between Tom and Lydia sets a standard for 'the great relationship', the linguistic event that marks its beginning is also a standard for an articulacy that is lived before it is contrived as a pattern of communication.

Other instances of felt articulacy can be cited from different sections of the novel, and involving different characters. One of the earliest scenes displaying real communication between Tom and the child Anna has both of them engaging in an invented language that completely and unselfconsciously expresses the feelings of each.

'Go away.'

'I'm *not* going away,' he shouted, irritated at last. 'Go yourself – hustle – stir thysen – hop.' And he pointed to the door. The child backed away from him, pale with fear. Then she gathered up courage, seeing him become patient.

'We don't live with *you*!' she said, thrusting forward her little head at him. 'You – you're – you're a bomakle.'

'A what?' he shouted.

Her voice wavered – but it came.

'A bomakle.'

'Ay, an' you're a comakle.'

She meditated. Then she hissed forward her head.

'I'm not.'

'Not what?'

'A comakle.'

'No more am I a bomakle.'
He was really cross. (p. 70)

Tom's irritation is seen through his initial attempt to finish
the exchange and defeat the child by means of a display of his
own dialect, drawing thereby on his instinctive sense of security
in occupying his own farm, own region, own language against
the little Polish girl. The string of verbs, 'Go yourself – hustle
– stir thysen – hop', is his endeavour to shut Anna out of the
conversation as much as it is a series of repeated commands to
leave the room. But Anna's response meets the challenge head-on.
She invents her own vocabulary, and with the word 'bomakle' finds
both an adequate expression for her anger and at the same time
seeks to exclude Tom from a linguistic encounter as he had sought
to exclude her. With Tom's 'Ay, an' you're a comakle', however,
Lawrence caps the conversation. Tom, with instinctive linguistic
flexibility, adopts Anna's new vocabulary, enters the world of
her language, and succeeds in insulting her with a meaningless
invented term. The fact that he is himself stung by the name
'bomakle' just as much as Anna is by 'comakle' provides the
ground for the genuine communication. Tom is not toying with
Anna. He is genuinely within the language he is exchanging with
her, and the emotions encapsulated in 'comakle' and 'bomakle'
are called up and expressed by and in the words for the adult
as much as for the child. At the same time, Tom's readiness
to abandon his normal idiom for an invented one, and to find
it, apparently, equally expressive, indicates something about the
frailty of his hold on 'the spoken world': language is a relatively
recent acquisition for the Brangwen men, and emotions under
pressure can find release in 'comakle' as readily as in 'That's her'.

With the next generation, we have a new version of 'the
great relationship' and new voices to express the experience
of it. Will and Anna are made to rely on the narrative voice
as much as Tom and Lydia did, for their emotions, as already
seen, are frequently beyond their linguistic grasp. This is particularly the case in the chapter 'Anna Victrix'. The reliance on
narrative, however, allows Lawrence to highlight the shifts in the
patterns between 'the heated, blind intercourse of farm-life' and
'the spoken world beyond', and to do so through a focus on the
spoken word.

Will Brangwen went home without having seen his uncle. He held his hot face to the rain, and walked on in a trance. 'I love you, Will, I love you.' The words repeated themselves endlessly. The veils had ripped and issued him naked into the endless space, and he shuddered. . . . 'I love you, Will, I love you.' He trembled with fear as the words beat in his heart again. And he dared not think of her face, of her eyes which shone, and of her strange, transfigured face. (p. 120)

Will is literally walking away from the farm at this point, leaving the uncle whom he has not seen 'sweating with pain, with the horror of being old, with the agony of having to relinquish what was life to him' (p. 120). Yet though he leaves a passion behind to be confronted by Tom, his own passion, his fear and excitement, goes with him, illuminated and fed by the spoken words 'I love you, Will, I love you'. The veils that have been 'ripped', the nakedness he is experiencing, are a consequence of the voice of a woman, and the power of her words reaches 'beyond' the spoken event itself into the world of his everyday life and his mental and emotional assumptions. His visits to the 'farm-life' have aroused a spoken passion in Anna, and the words that have expressed that passion now 'beat in his heart' with an emotion of their own, displaying to him his own lack of readiness for passion and his fear.

The pattern of Will's dilemma is repeated in the final sentence of the quotation. He is thinking of what he dare not think, and the circularity of his thoughts finds enactment in the series of co-ordinate groups complementing the verbal form plus extension 'think of': 'her face', 'her eyes which shone', 'her strange, transfigured face'. The first is a simple nominal group, comprising modifier and headword. The second, however, while promising to follow the same pattern as the first, is extended by a subordinate adjectival clause, 'which shone'. The 'eyes' that were already a sign that Will's mind is running over what he 'dared not think of' are given a radiance and a power beyond their mere existence. They exist, and actively exist through their capacity to disrupt the expected syntactical structure. Yet another disruption occurs with the third group, for Lawrence repeats the first item of the series rather than choosing a different feature – mouth, say, or hair. In doing so he does literally transfigure 'her face' by the addition of two extra modifiers, 'strange' and 'transfigured'. But he also enforces the pattern into which Will's mind has been trapped: he always returns to the face of which he dare not think, and each time he returns it is to find it expressed with still greater power and still greater capacity to terrify. If subordination expresses the connectedness of thought, co-ordination, as here, can present the mental and emotional whirlpools that are produced by the shock of new experience and new linguistic stimuli.

One final example of the rudimentary language of the characters presenting emotion with perfect articulacy concerns the death of Tom Brangwen. This is a scene of considerable significance for many threads of the novel, and in so far as Tom has been the first of the Brangwens to find a voice and to move a step away from blind inarticulacy we also find some resolution of the language debate. Here, as at other key points, Lawrence makes the human voice prominent, both through commentary and through the reactions of other characters. This time, the voice is Lydia's.

Water was running in and out of the scullery. She paddled through barefoot, to see. Water was bubbling fiercely under the outer door. She was afraid. Then something washed against her, something twined under her foot. It was the riding whip. On the table were the rug and the cushion and the parcel from the gig.

He had come home.

'Tom!' she called, afraid of her own voice.

She opened the door. Water ran in with a horrid sound. Everywhere was moving water, a sound of waters.

'Tom!' she cried, standing in her nightdress with the candle, calling into the darkness and the flood out of the doorway.

'Tom! Tom!'

And she listened. Fred appeared behind her, in trousers and shirt.

'Where is he?' he asked.

He looked at the flood, then at his mother. She seemed small and uncanny, elvish in her nightdress.

'Go upstairs,' he said. 'He'll be in th' stable.'

'To–om! To–om!' cried the elderly woman, with a long, unnatural, penetrating call that chilled her son to the marrow. He quickly pulled on his boots and his coat.

'Go upstairs, mother,' he said, 'I'll go an' see where he is.'

'To–om! To–o–om!' rang out the shrill, unearthly cry of the small woman. There was only the noise of water and the mooing of uneasy cattle, and the long yelping of the dog, clamouring in the darkness.

Fred Brangwen splashed out into the flood with a lantern. His mother stood on a chair in the doorway, watching him go. It was all water, water, running flashing under the lantern.

'Tom! Tom! To–o–om!' came her long, unnatural cry, ringing over the night. It made her son feel cold in his soul. . . .

'It's getting higher,' said Tilly. 'Hasn't master come in?'

Mrs Brangwen did not hear.

'Isn't he the–ere?' she called, in her far-reaching, terrifying voice.

'No,' came the short answer out of the night.

'Go and loo–ok for him.'

His mother's voice nearly drove the youth mad. . . .

'Is he th–e-ere?' came the maddening cry of the mother.

'No,' was the sharp answer.

'To–om – To–o–om!' came the piercing, free, unearthly call. It seemed high and supernatural, almost pure. Fred Brangwen hated it. It nearly drove him mad. So awfully it sang out, almost like a song.

The water was flowing fuller into the house.

'You'd better go up to Beeby's and bring him and Arthur down, and tell Mrs Beeby to fetch Wilkinson,' said Fred to Tilly. He forced his mother to go upstairs.

'I know your father is drowned,' she said, in curious dismay.

The flood rose through the night, till it washed the kettle off the hob in the kitchen. Mrs Brangwen sat alone at a window upstairs. She called no more. The men were busy with the pigs and the cattle. They were coming with a boat for her. (pp. 247–9)

The feel of the generations of Brangwens is strong here as Tom comes 'home': the kitchen is where he prepared for his proposal to Lydia; the cattle in the darkness recall those to which he carried the child Anna to calm her; Lydia looking into the rain after Tom recalls Tom himself looking in anguish

after Anna and Will, courting; the canal that rises to drown him
is one of the sources of Brangwen prosperity. Above all, Lydia
looking out into the darkness is a version of the activity of the
women since the first generations of Brangwens, the women who
'looked out from the heated, blind intercourse of farm-life, to
the spoken world beyond' (p. 8). But she is looking not for a
fulfilment that is 'beyond' her, but for the return of a fulfilment
that has already been hers. She does not 'strain to listen' for 'the
lips and mind of the world speaking and giving utterance' (p. 8),
but for any sound at all that is not 'the sound of waters'. It is
her own cry, the haunting 'To–o–om', that replaces the 'magic
language' that earlier women yearned for, and what she hears
back are only the sounds of 'farm-life' that have accompanied
each generation of the family through the stages of existence.

Lawrence emphasises Lydia's voice in several ways. One, of
course, is its effect on Fred: his behaviour, and Tilly's, contrast
with Lydia's, the ordinariness of their language ('I'll go an' see
where he is', 'Hasn't master come in?') showing up the intensity
of hers. The overwhelming sounds of the flood are also ranged
against the single-minded clarity of her calling. Her repetition of
'Tom' is matched by Lawrence's more varied repetition of 'water'
– 'Water was bubbling', 'Water ran', 'a sound of waters', 'It was
all water, water' – as if the swirling uncontrolled water will enter
every sentence, occupy every grammatical position. The only firm
item in the scene is Lydia's calling. And, of course, what is called is
simply a man's name. Articulacy, the 'magic' quality of language,
has been reduced to a single syllable, stretched out in anxiety to
encompass all the emotions of a lifetime – loss, despair, renewal,
love, doubt, security, and the awful knowledge of renewed loss.
'That's her' and 'I love you, Will, I love you' find their inevitable
last phase in 'To–o–om'.

The instinctive knowledge of death and loss, that makes the
calm of 'I know your father is drowned' so resolutely final, is
accessible only through character and the language of character.
Yet our access to character, that makes us read Lydia's calling
in this particular way, has been provided by the whole narrative
strategy from the first pages of the novel, and by the handling of
the language debate within the treatment of men, women and the
context of their lives. When the men busy themselves with 'the pigs
and the cattle', they are continuing with the kinds of activities that

Brangwen men have always carried out, blindly and for profit. The heated intercourse goes on, whether articulated or not. But when Lydia sits alone at her window, and calls 'no more', she has lapsed from expression to silence, from looking out in the expectation of there being something to hear, something to respond to, to the state of there being nothing left to express. Her silence is not the pre-linguistic silence of inarticulacy, but of everything having now been said.

Tom's death, however, is only a stage in the life of *The Rainbow*. As succeeding generations take over, the farm becomes more remote to the story, and language is more and more taken for granted as an acquisition of the characters. Ursula, as she moves out into the world that was once 'beyond', meets and hears a range of voices for which the earlier women could only strain to listen. As she does so it becomes increasingly clear that the 'magic language', the language that was associated with influence, with power, with knowledge, with religion (pp. 9–10), is always elusive. The more voices there are to hear, the less magic there is in any of them. We have already seen in Chapter 5 the insincerity that articulacy makes possible in characters such as Winifred Inger and uncle Tom Brangwen. Theirs is an artificial articulacy that is based not in real lived experience and emotions but in experience only of language itself. The structures and conventions of language permit and encourage detachment from the 'heated, blind intercourse' of emotional involvement. The true potential of language for the development of human understanding, for the 'achieving of a pure relationship between ourselves and the living universe about us' (*Phoenix*, p. 528), is betrayed when language is used to hide, either from oneself or from others, and what is present in Winifred and uncle Tom finds its culmination in *Women in Love* with the linguistically decadent articulacy of Breadalby and the Cafe Pompadour.

As Ursula moves out, she encounters more varied experiences than any of her predecessors, but she also encounters less and less meaning. The resonance of objects, like the kettle that is 'washed . . . off the hob in the kitchen' (p. 249), and therefore of the language that describes them, is lost when the 'peg' for 'Standard Five teacher' (p. 371) or the 'cottage in Sussex' (p. 463) is encountered, left, and never thought of again. This language loses the capacity not only for emotional engagement but for relating lived experience to the life of the past, to history, to a continuing social reality that gives significance to the thoughts and actions of the individual. Yet the wider, modern world cannot be avoided. Lawrence would have been an anachronism had his intention in *The Rainbow* been to praise the past of Marsh Farm at the expense of engagement with contemporary society. But the language debate takes on a different form. Ursula's linguistic dilemma is to find a voice that will deal with the increasingly 'spoken' world without distorting herself.

She does not do so, though she does finally avoid the seductive examples of her mother, of Winifred, and of Anton Skrebensky. But Lawrence does so on her behalf. Just as the early Brangwens were pre-linguistic in their context, so Ursula at the very end of the novel is in hers. She has put aside various forms of life, and with them the forms of language that they impose on the free individual: 'Her husband was John Smith, loader. We reckoned him as a loader, he reckoned himself as a loader, and so she knew he represented his job.' (pp. 348–9) Now she waits. The early Brangwens were innocently pre-linguistic, knowing only one continuing flow of experience, while Ursula comes to her pre-linguistic state through the knowledge and experience of articulacy in the modern world. When Lawrence speaks on her behalf, it is not over and above her, as the opening pages of the novel are over and above each individual Brangwen, but with her full knowledge and consent.

The last pages of *The Rainbow*, over which Lawrence spent so much trouble, are the culmination both of the role of the Brangwen women, looking out, and of the language debate. The 'spoken world' they looked to, after all, has been both encountered and missed by Ursula. Her last linguistic act in the novel is to write her letter of submission to Skrebensky. 'This letter she wrote, sentence by sentence, as if from her deepest, sincerest heart.' (pp. 485–6) Thereafter, she is spoken for by Lawrence as she goes through the traumatic experience with the horses, falls ill, realises that there will be no child and that 'she would not have gone to Skrebensky' (p. 494). As she sits watching at her window, she resembles those earlier nameless women who watched and listened, and Lydia looking for her lost fulfilment, and Anna, who looked out, saw the rainbow, and declined to 'travel any further' (p. 196). What Ursula sees is the real rainbow, but also a vision of what it is that the rainbow means.

> And the rainbow stood on the earth. She knew that the sordid people who crept hard-scaled and separate on the face of the world's corruption were living still, that the rainbow was arched in their blood and would quiver to life in their spirit, that they would cast off their horny covering of disintegration, that new, clean, naked bodies would issue to a new germination, to a new growth, rising to the light and the wind and the clean rain of heaven. She saw in the rainbow the earth's new architecture, the old, brittle corruption of houses swept away, the world built up in a living fabric of Truth, fitting to the over-arching heaven. (pp. 495–6)

This is stated with Ursula's knowledge and consent in so far as it is her knowledge that is being presented, albeit in a language that is not hers. She is the focus for both the seeing and the realisation, and would make these assertions herself had she the forms of language to do so. Yet there is something laboured here. Lawrence, in trying to present a language that crystallises the knowledge of a character who cannot yet aspire to the language for herself, has loaded the forms with too much self-importance. The vision is unconvincing. There is the relentless stream of significant modifiers ('sordid', 'hard-scaled', 'separate', 'horny', 'new', 'clean', 'living'). There are the straining rhythms of the prose: the long second sentence that builds rather obviously to a crescendo through the use of co-ordination – 'She knew that . . . that . . . that . . . that . . . ' – and of co-ordination within co-ordination – 'to a new germination . . . to a new growth . . . to the light and the wind and the clean rain . . . '. And the attempt to use 'architecture' as the link between the spiritual and the actual seems simple-minded. How can 'houses and factories' (p. 495) be replaced by a spiritual architecture 'built up in a living fabric of Truth'? Here, if anywhere, is language that locates itself not in lived experience, or even in lived imagination, but in the forces and choices of its own construction.

To this extent, the end of *The Rainbow* is a disappointment, and, as we know, was so to Lawrence as well. But as a last stage in the treatment of language, what Lawrence makes Ursula know is far more convincing. Throughout the novel we have seen the play of language that has done justice to the 'heated, blind intercourse', shown its strengths and limitations in relation to the elusive 'spoken world beyond'. And we have seen, too, how Lawrence's focus upon language itself has contributed to the creation of character and character relations: articulacy and lived experience have together been crucial factors in rendering men and women in the context of each other and of their social realities. The 'magic language' has been listened for by the women, and never heard, while the men have been 'aware of something standing above . . . and beyond . . . in the distance' (p. 7). Meanwhile language has been generated by the friction between living and looking out. Language, like Ursula's rainbow, is 'arched' in the 'blood' of men and women and will 'quiver to life in their spirit'. The rainbow she sees is the language for which she is waiting, having been rendered dumb after the many voices she has learned. The women '*looked*' out to the '*spoken*' world beyond. Ursula looks out across the world's corruption, which she has experienced in all its spoken forms, and sees the language that can only be just to its subjects when it is based in the clarity and nakedness of lived experience, in 'a living fabric of Truth'. This is not only Lawrence's 'language for the feelings' (*Phoenix*, p. 757). It is language for 'living', and the knowledge of it is arrived at after the ebb and flow between life and language that has been the experience of the novel.

And of course the language that is the rainbow is also *The Rainbow*. The forms of language that strive to '*honour*' the 'true and vivid relationships' of mankind (*Phoenix*, p. 530) are the forms that constitute the art of the novelist. If 'The novel is the perfect medium for revealing to us the changing rainbow of our living relationships' (*Phoenix*, p. 532), the vision that is given to Ursula is one that reveals her position as akin to the novelist himself. She has been able to enter and do justice to the forms of living without, finally, losing her individuality. She has experienced the pattern, and can now see it whole. The next stage will be to speak what she can see. Appropriately, she waits at the brink of articulacy as the novel itself lapses into silence. When she is recovered, in *Women in Love*, it is to have surrendered her linguistic inheritance to Rupert Birkin.

8   The Language of Poetry

> I remember the slightly self-conscious Sunday afternoon, when
> I was nineteen, and I "composed" my first two "poems." One
> was to *Guelder-roses*, and one to *Campions*, and most young
> ladies would have done better: at least I hope so. But I thought
> the effusions very nice, and so did Miriam. (*Complete Poems*,
> II, 849)

Lawrence wrote this in May 1928, after the publication of seven
volumes of poetry during the years since he was nineteen, and with
a collected edition in preparation. He could afford to be dismissive
about his first efforts, and about his first attempt at publication:
'Myself, I had offered the little poem *Study* to the Nottingham
University Magazine, but they returned it.' (*Complete Poems*,
II, 851) His first appearance in a serious literary magazine had
been as a poet when Ford Madox Ford accepted three poems for
the *English Review*, and published them in November 1909. The
poem 'Snap-Dragon', written in the summer of 1907, two years
after his first 'compositions', was published in the *English Review*
in June 1912 and subsequently in Edward Marsh's *Georgian Poetry
1911–1912*, which also appeared in 1912 and was continuing to
provide Lawrence with royalties in January 1914 (*Letters*, II, 140).
By the end of his life, the moral danger of his poetry was sufficient
for the English authorities to censor the collection *Pansies* before
its publication in 1929:

> Some of the poems are perforce omitted – about a dozen
> from the bunch. When Scotland Yard seized the MS. in the
> post, at the order of the Home Secretary, no doubt there was a
> rush of detectives, postmen, and Home Office clerks and heads,
> to pick out the most lurid blossoms. They must have been very

disappointed. When I now read down the list of the omitted poems, and recall the dozen amusing, not terribly important bits of pansies which have had to stay out of print for fear a policeman might put his foot on them, I can only grin once more to think of the nanny-goat, nanny-goat-in-a-white-petticoat silliness of it all. (*Complete Poems*, I, 423)

Poetry was part of Lawrence's life from his very earliest years. Nonconformist hymns, as we have seen, were an important influence in shaping his consciousness – more so, he confesses, even than those 'poems which have meant most to me, like Wordworth's "Ode to Immortality" and Keats's Odes, and pieces of *Macbeth* or *As You Like It* or *Midsummer Night's Dream*, and Goethe's lyrics . . . – all these lovely poems which after all give the ultimate shape to one's life; all these lovely poems woven deep into a man's consciousness' (*Phoenix II*, 597). Much of his early reading, too, had been of poetry – Shakespeare, Blake, Longfellow, Tennyson, Browning, Palgrave's *Golden Treasury of Songs and Lyrics*.[1] He also taught poetry as part of his duties in Croydon, as his headmaster at the time recalled in 1951:

Lawrence's choice of verse for class study was, for the time, unorthodox. He would have none of the "We are seven etc" category. Nor would he tolerate any with what he called "a sniff of moral imposition." I found entered in his records such selections as "The Assyrian Came Down" (Byron), "The Bells of Shandon" (Mahony), "Go fetch to me a pint of wine" (Burns). He considered that the best approach to poetry for young people was through rhythm and the ring of words rather than the evasive appeal of an unreal and abstract morality. (Nehls, pp. 87–8)

All three of the poems first published by Ford were written during Lawrence's time in Croydon. 'Dreams Old and Nascent' and 'Discipline' both concern classroom teaching, and 'Baby Movements' was about the new daughter of his Croydon landlady, Mrs Marie Jones. But it was not until his contact with Edward Marsh in the autumn of 1912 that Lawrence was obliged to enter into debate about the nature of poetry, and to justify his own opinions and practice.

Marsh had read 'Snap-Dragon' in the *English Review* and decided it would be right for his *Georgian Poetry* anthology. 'It's far from perfect,' he wrote to Walter De La Mare (another contributor to the volume), 'but like his two novels it seems to me to have elements of great and rather strange power and beauty.'[2] Marsh preferred poetry to be 'written on some formal principle which I could discern, and from which it departed, if at all, only for the sake of some special effect, and not because the lazy or too impetuous writer had found observance difficult or irksome'. Apart from this he looked for poetry that was 'intelligible, musical and racy'.[3] It is easy to see with 'Snap-Dragon' why Marsh found it acceptable. There is enough of the traditional in its poetic form and in Lawrence's handling of language for a reader like Marsh to be able to 'discern' its 'formal principle'.

> She bade me follow to her garden, where
> The mellow sunlight stood as in a cup
> Between the old grey walls; I did not dare
> To raise my face, I did not dare look up,
> Lest her bright eyes like sparrows should fly in
> My windows of discovery, and shrill 'Sin.'
>
> (*Complete Poems*, I, 122–6)

The language chosen is deliberately low-key in this first verse of the poem. Some of it is archaic – 'bade', 'Lest' – and some self-consciously poetical – 'mellow sunlight', 'the old grey walls', 'her bright eyes like sparrows'. If there is variation in rhythm through Lawrence's use of punctuation – the run-on lines, the late pause in the first line followed by expansiveness as he describes the 'sunlight' over almost two lines before the heavy semi-colon in the third – there is also the security of a fixed rhyme scheme. The phrase 'as in a cup', however, is rather awkward, and seems to be there only for the rhyme with 'up'. The suggestion of confinement with 'cup' also contradicts the rhythmic expanse of the line that Lawrence has contrived through the use of punctuation. Most significantly, 'as in a cup' plays no part in the extended chain of subordination that is commonly an essential structural feature of Lawrence's writing. Here, 'where/The Mellow sunlight stood' is an adjectival clause dependent upon 'garden', and 'Between the old grey walls' an adverbial phrase dependent upon 'stood'. But within this verse 'as in a cup' has no part in the pattern: it is a simile that develops the appearance of the sunlight, and nothing more. Lawrence picks up the image again with 'brown bowl' and 'her cup' in the sixth verse, but this does not help to tie it into the structure of verse one. It leads to nothing: nothing depends upon it, which emphasises its being there just for the rhyme. This slackness in the syntactical arrangement of the poetry contrasts strikingly with later verses of the poem. However, the repetition – 'I did not dare . . . I did not dare' – is a foretaste of the techniques that will appear as the poem progresses. And there are surprises. The 'eyes like sparrows' is unusual, but is the beginning of the bird imagery that is to be developed. The poet's 'windows of discovery' make him something apart from the girl whose behaviour seems unselfconscious and natural, and give him more in common, in fact, with the 'old grey walls' than with the brightness of her eyes. The forcing of the adjective 'shrill' into service as a verb, which is not a normal modern usage, draws startling attention to the sense of shame and fear of discovery that, at the moment, the poet is desperate to hide.

Later verses pick up what has been established here, and also form a strong contrast in so far as the poet's developing self-confidence is conveyed through much stronger and more daring use of language.

> Then I laughed in the dark of my heart, I did exult
> Like a sudden chuckling of music. I bade her eyes
> Meet mine, I opened her helpless eyes to consult
> Their fear, their shame, their joy that underlies
> Defeat in such a battle. In the dark of her eyes
> My heart was fierce to make her laughter rise.

The grammar and diction of this verse are far more robust. This is most immediately apparent in the choice of verbs. Where in the first verse the girl 'bade', the sunlight 'stood' while the poet 'did not dare look up', now it is 'I' who 'laughed', who 'did exult', who 'bade' and 'opened'. In the first line, the presence of a second main clause 'I did exult . . . ' in parallel to 'I laughed . . . ' emphasises the fact that it is the poet himself who is now the prime mover in the scene, and the expansion of the simple past 'I laughed' of the first clause to auxiliary plus infinitive, 'did exult', in the second, underlines the joy of self-assertion: he not only controls the verbs, he draws them out and relishes them! He is even able to adopt her verb 'bade' from the first verse, where it was part of the tone of conventional poetic respectability, and throw it back in defiance in a context of verbal challenge. The linguistic status quo of the poem, we realise, has been overturned, and the poet's sense of triumph is imposed through his reordering of items of his own poetic expression.

The second sentence is particularly interesting. Again we have two main clauses – 'I bade . . . ' and 'I opened . . . ' – but here they are made more pointedly parallel by giving each verb the same repeated complement, 'her eyes'. The addition of a modifier, 'helpless', at their second appearance stresses their status – their helplessness is an essential feature of the girl's new passivity in the face of the poet's assertiveness. This passivity is maintained in the infinitive 'to consult', which contrasts with the energy of the verbs assigned to the 'I'. The structure of the sentence relies heavily upon subordination. The complement 'her helpless eyes' governs the whole of the rest of the sentence. The three nominal groups of the fourth line, 'Their fear, their shame, their joy', all depend upon the verb 'consult' which itself depends upon 'eyes'. The final exultant 'that underlies/Defeat in such a battle' is dependent upon the third of the co-ordinating nominal groups, 'their joy'. A ranking has been established through the action of the poem, through the largely unspoken emotional communication that has been going on between man and girl. He has moved from subordinate to superior, while she has come to recognise his mastery and, as he sees it, to experience 'joy' in the recognition. The battle of man/woman relationships, remarked on in Chapter 2, is flatteringly worked out for the man in this early poem. What is significant, though, is Lawrence's manipulation of language that turns the tentative, self-conscious diction and structures of verse one into the free-flowing patterns of repetition and subordination that mark the song of conquest of the final verses.

But Marsh also found the poem 'far from perfect', and if we look at the subsequent correspondence between Marsh and Lawrence we can see both what he meant by 'far from perfect' and why Lawrence could not for long remain within the constraints of the Georgian coterie. Marsh, apparently, found Lawrence's work particularly loose in terms of rhythm, and held up James Elroy

Flecker's 'The Golden Journey to Samarkand' as rhythmically correct. Flecker specialised in tight and unvarying rhythms held in place by strong, rather predictable rhymes.

> Sweet to ride forth at evening from the wells,
>   When shadows pass gigantic on the sand,
> And softly through the silence beat the bells
>   Along the Golden Road to Samarkand.

> We travel not for trafficking alone:
>   By hotter winds our fiery hearts are fanned:
> For lust of knowing what should not be known
>   We make the Golden Journey to Samarkand.

What is more, Flecker's subjects were not, like Lawrence's, the spiritual and emotional events behind everyday experience, but concerned the unusual, the heroic, the exotic. Lawrence wrote to Lady Cynthia Asquith in August, 1913:

> *The Golden Journey to Samarkand.* You knew it climbed Parnassus *en route*? I shall write a book called 'The Poet's Geographer' one day. – By the way, Mr Marsh will hold it as a personal favour if I will take more care of my rhythms. Poor things, they go cackling round like a poultry farm. – But he told it me – I mean Eddie-dear – in a letter. He thinks I'm too Rag-Time: not that he says so. But if you'll believe me, that 'Golden Journey to Samarkand' only took place on paper – no matter who went to Asia Minor. (*Letters*, II, 62)

What this implies is a distinction in Lawrence's mind between correct but lifeless verse, and the tumultuousness of lived experience that demands an unsettled rhythmic expression. It is a distinction he made in a letter to Marsh himself in the same month.

> – I think you will find my verse smoother – not because I consciously attend to rhythms, but because I am no longer so criss-crossy in myself. I think, don't you know, that my rhythms fit my mood pretty well, in the verse. And if the mood is out of joint, the rhythm often is. I have always tried to get an emotion out in its own course, without altering it. It needs the finest

instinct imaginable, much finer than the skill of the craftsmen. That Japanese Yone Noguchi tried it. He doesn't quite bring it off. Often I don't – sometimes I do. Sometimes Whitman is perfect. Remember skilled verse is dead in fifty years – I am thinking of your admiration of Flecker. (*Letters*, II, 61)

On 18 November 1913, Lawrence again wrote to Marsh in continuation of the debate, developing his remarks about rhythm and feeling:

You *are* wrong. It makes me open my eyes. I think I read my poetry more by length than by stress – as a matter of movements in space than footsteps hitting the earth. . . . I think more of a bird with broad wings flying and lapsing through the air, than anything, when I think of metre. . . . It all depends on the *pause* – the natural pause, the natural *lingering* of the voice according to the feeling – it is the hidden *emotional* pattern that makes poetry, not the obvious form. (*Letters*, II, 102–4)

And he added an attack on March's competence as a reader of poetry. 'Feeling,' he says,

doesn't depend on the ear, particularly, but on the sensitive soul. And the ear gets a habit, and becomes master, when the ebbing and lifting emotion should be master, and the ear the transmitter. If your ear has got stiff and a bit mechanical, *don't* blame my poetry. That's why you like *Golden Journey to Samarkand* – it fits your habituated ear, and your feeling crouches subservient and a bit pathetic. 'It satisfies my ear' you say. Well, I don't write for your ear. This is the constant war, I reckon, between new expression and the habituated, mechanical transmitters and receivers of the human constitution. (*Letters*, II, 104)

If we look at an example of the poetry Lawrence had been writing during the period before his correspondence with Marsh, we shall see more precisely what he meant by expressions like metre 'Lying and lapsing' and 'the hidden emotional pattern that makes poetry'. 'Bei Hennef' was written in May 1912, the month in which he left England with Frieda. The poem was first published in *Love Poems and Others* in 1913, but is unlike most of the poems in the collection in being addressed to Frieda and in being written in a free, unrhymed form. Lawrence, in his 1928 Preface to his *Collected Poems*, says that the poem 'starts the new cycle' after 'the death-experience' of life in England (*Complete Poems*, I, 28). He describes the scene of the poem in a letter to Frieda from Hennef as he waits for his train:

> I am sitting like a sad swain beside a nice, twittering little river, waiting for the twilight to drop, and my last train to come. . . . It's getting dark. Now, for the first time during today, my detachment leaves me, and I know I only love you. The rest is nothing at all. And the promise of life with you is all richness. Now I know. (*Letters*, I, 398)

Already in the letter we can see some of the items that will be significant features of the poem: the details of the scene, like the 'twittering' river and the 'twilight'; and the expression, like the emphasis on the simplicity of 'I know'. What is absent in the poem is the touch of humour in 'sad swain' and 'nice', as well as the fact that Lawrence is waiting for a train. Instead, he first of all allows the scene to speak for itself before suggesting any hint of personal emotion:

> The little river twittering in the twilight,
> The wan, wandering look of the pale sky,
> This is almost bliss.

(*Complete Poems*, I, 203)

The pattern of the poetry relies initially on alliteration, not only the very apparent 'twittering . . . twilight' and 'wan, wandering', but the less obvious 'little . . . twittering' and virtually the entire last line 'This is . . . bliss'. It is only with the third line that the emotion that has been underlying the description (and, in the case of 'wan' and 'pale', only just being kept within the confines of description) is made explicit, and the pattern of feeling, the significance of 'almost', gathers into focus. The attractive little scene is not quite complete for him. This is reflected in the grammatical arrangement of the lines. Each of the first two lines aspires to become the main clause of the sentence, and each has a verbal form that could have become the main verb – 'twittering' and 'wandering' – but that completeness is denied and both lines are summarised in the pronoun 'This' in order to achieve the grammatical resolution that itself expresses incompleteness: 'This is almost bliss.' We have a 'hidden *emotional* pattern' of incompleteness that emerges with the straightforward statement in the third line, and we have a rhythmical arrangement that depends upon not only alliteration and repetition to sustain its flights but on grammatical frustration for an incompleteness that awaits completion in the rest of the poem.

And the rest of the poem almost provides rhythmic satisfaction – or rather it almost provides a series of rhythmic satisfactions.

> And everything shut up and gone to sleep,
> All the troubles and anxieties and pain
>   Gone under the twilight.
>
> Only the twilight now, and the soft 'Sh!' of the river
>   That will last for ever.

The rhythm of these two verses is one of soothing, as the calm of the scene is brought out in terms of the poet's state of mind. The 'twittering' is forgotten, to be replaced by the 'soft "Sh! of the river' that has been suggested not by 'twittering' but by the sounds of 'This is almost bliss'. Lawrence is already tieing his verses together not through rhyme but through a more intricate pattern of repeated sounds. Individual words, and even parts of words, are made to generate themselves as the poem builds up the rhythms of feeling that accompany the scene: 'twilight' from the first verse, followed by 'under the twilight' and 'Only the twilight'; 'gone' and 'Gone'; 'everything', 'ever' and its half-rhyme 'river'. Yet the quietening of the poet's soul remains incomplete, for both these verses lack the grammatical resolution even of the first. Each suggests a slowing down towards resolution, with the repeated 'gone' and the finality of 'for ever'. Yet neither verse is grammatically complete for neither is a sentence in its own right. The second lacks a main verb, such as the 'is' of the first verse ('And everything *is* shut up'), while the third requires something stronger – '*There is* only the twilight', for example. In other words, the illusion of completeness, of being quite calm and settled, is presented, but the hidden emotion that is governing the underlying grammar of the poem remains in suspense, unready for resolution, in a state of 'almost'.

Rhythmic and emotional satisfaction draw even closer in the fourth verse.

> And at last I know my love for you is here;
> I can see it all, it is whole like the twilight,
> It is large, so large, I could not see it before,
> Because of the little lights and flickers and interruptions,
>   Troubles, anxieties and pains.

Again there is the tieing together through repetition: 'at last' and the verb 'last' of the third verse; 'twilight' again; 'little' from the first verse; and, within the verse, 'see' and 'large'. New linguistic items, however, draw attention to themselves through their very newness: 'I know', 'my love', 'here', 'see', 'large'. The poet has apparently gained the stillness of spirit he never quite achieved in the preceding verses. The concentration is on 'here', the place and moment of 'the new cycle', and he can forget 'the death-experience'. He is, 'for the first time', no longer detached and is able, therefore, to 'know' his own emotions. But there is repetition of grammatical structures as well as of sounds in this verse, and that also has an effect on the 'ebbing and lifting' of the emotion. The line 'Because of the little lights and flickers and interruptions' recalls in its structure 'All the troubles and anxieties and pain'. At the moment of forgetting, of seeing his love 'whole like the twilight', the poet is reminded of what prevented him from seeing it, and the rhythm that in the second verse was soothing away pain now threatens to restore it to him. The parallel structures of the lines (*a* and *b* and *c* in each case) straightaway brings back the qualities that constituted the *a*, *b* and *c* in the second verse: 'Troubles, anxieties and pains'. The consequence is that this verse, that has been steadily building up a vision of wholeness through repetition of its own – 'I can see it all . . . It is large, so large, I could not see it before' – is compelled to end with what has all along inhibited wholeness: it ends with an 'interruption'.

With the fifth verse the poet makes a radical structural change

and adopts a highly self-conscious style that depends upon almost
exactly repeated syntactical units in order to express his love, his
emotion.

> You are the call and I am the answer,
> You are the wish, and I the fulfilment,
> You are the night, and I the day.
>> What else? it is perfect enough.
>> It is perfectly complete,
>> You and I,
>> What more – ?

Throughout the poem so far there has been a closer relation
between the poet's genuine underlying emotion and the grammar
of the writing than between the emotion and the scene that
purports to encapsulate it. The poem, in other words, has dealt
with incompleteness, both emotional and linguistic, rather than
wholeness. It is appropriate, then, that the first of the three parallel
structures should express love in terms of language: the call and
the answer. The second expresses it in terms of the spiritual life,
of the desires and satisfactions for which language speaks. The
third makes the jump from the emotional patterns of individuals
to the repeating patterns of the universe, the cosmic events that
bring about night and day. And this structure does indeed express
completeness. In the first line one main clause ('You are the call')
is exactly matched by a second ('I am the answer'). With the next
line, the two main verbs 'are' and 'am' are reduced to the single
'are', implying an even closer relation between the two halves:
both are able to share the same verb. While the double repetition
suggests resolution, it also suggests extension. A linguistic arrangement, once begun and emphasised by repetition, is difficult to alter
without bathos. Three almost identical lines that expand the scope
of the poet's love to the level of cosmic movements are difficult to
conclude. So Lawrence asks: 'What else?' and the question itself
brings about the sense of anti-climax that it attempts to confront.
What else *can* there be, after 'You are the night, and I the day'?
And as soon as the statement 'it is perfect enough' is made, we
know that the rhythmic and grammatical interruption of 'What
else?' was indicative of the remaining underlying unease. The
poet, for all his attempts at securing rhythmic satisfaction, is

back at the stage of 'almost' bliss. Even the repetition of the adjective 'perfect' in the adverb 'perfectly' cannot compensate for the rhythmic lapse of 'What else?' or the awful admission 'it is perfect enough'. Indeed, the repetition of 'perfect' in fact carries with it the reminder of 'enough', and thereby devalues the perfect of 'perfectly complete'. The shift to the self-consciously lyrical in expression has been abandoned as suddenly as it began, and the language is left seeming tentative and inconclusive: 'What else? . . . You and I,/What more – ?'

Lawrence, then, by the end of this verse, has reduced the language of the poem to the point of collapse: the retreating line lengths, the lack of flow in the lines, the grammatically incoherent attempt at a last sentence – 'It is perfectly complete,/You and I,/What more – ?' That this is so is cruelly and immediately endorsed by the last line of the poem: 'Strange, how we suffer in spite of this!' The language has recovered to an almost conversational level, and in doing so it stresses the breakdown that was taking place over the preceding four lines. And yet the recovery, far from expressing a matching emotional satisfaction, actually states clearly for the first time the real emotions of the poem: dissatisfaction, incompleteness, bewilderment. The long perspective that the poem has taken on the poet's emotion is brought finally into focus with the realisation that Lawrence is dealing not with a happiness that seems about to be his, but with one that is just failing to be his. The language and poetic strategies adopted are those that can tease out the feelings that belong to 'almost', not to 'bliss'. The phrase 'in spite of this' is particularly telling in this respect, for it points both to the surface attempt the poem makes to see emotion clearly and to the underlying emotion that actually governs the poem's structure and expression. The demonstrative pronoun 'this' must be understood as the poet's 'knowing' and 'seeing' his love, his assurance that 'You are the night, and I the day', and his confidence that 'It is perfectly complete'. But the poetic context he has constructed for these items so undermines them that his 'in spite' has also to be read as 'because'. The very source of the poet's potential happiness is also the source of his dissatisfaction, and 'this' is the whole poetic endeavour that has given true expression to a complex of emotions.

Lawrence, in rearranging his work for the 1928 *Collected Poems*, moved 'Bei Hennef' into the *Look! We Have Come*

Through! sequence, where the 'Lying and lapsing' of the relationship between himself and Frieda is given the fullest exploration through poems of extraordinary rhythmic freedom and emotional frankness. As Edward Marsh later put it, Lawrence 'was too great and strange for the likes of me'.[4] The Lawrence who could satisfy Marsh had been superseded even as Marsh published 'Snap-Dragon', and his views on poetry rapidly moved further and further away from those of his Georgian contemporaries.

Those views are forcefully put in an essay from August 1919 called 'Poetry of the Present', which became the preface to the American edition of *New Poems*. Lawrence writes with the assurance of some seven years of poetic development and practice, and what he has to say is clearly based on his under-standing of the kind of poetry he had been writing since leaving England in 1912. Central to his argument is a distinction between two kinds of poetry. First, there is traditional poetry, such as the 'treasured gem-like lyrics of Shelley and Keats', that Lawrence calls 'The poetry of the beginning and the poetry of the end'. By this he means that the poetry does not itself enact change. Rather, it is written from a perspective of stillness which can look undisturbed at what has been or what is to come. Because of this, such poetry has the assurance to be finished and whole, a single self-sufficient work. It 'is of the nature of all that is complete and consummate'.[5] The second kind of poetry is that which is 'at hand', is of 'the immediate present', and which has 'no perfection, no consummation, nothing finished' (*Complete Poems*, I, 181–2). It is this second kind that Lawrence sees as his own, and the bulk of the essay is given to expanding his sense of the poetry of the 'immediate moment'. One of its main characteristics, and a source of its superiority, is that it is closer to the real and changeable state of life itself, and, like his expectation of the novel form, can therefore do justice to the 'relatedness' of all things.

Do not ask for the qualities of the unfading timeless gems. Ask for the whiteness which is the seethe of mud, ask for that incipient putrescence which is the skies falling, ask for the never-pausing, never-ceasing life itself. There must be mutation, swifter than iridescence, haste, not rest, come-and-go, not fixity, inconclusiveness, immediacy, the quality of life itself, without dénouement or close. There must be the rapid momentaneous association of things which meet and pass on the forever incalculable journey of creation: everything left in its own rapid, fluid relationship with the rest of things. (*Complete Poems*, I, 183)

Lack of 'Ixity', 'inconclusiveness', 'immediacy', which are significant features of both the structure and the expression of a poem like 'Bei Hennef', naturally make a difference to the practice of poetry. The texture of poetic language, the manipulation of pace, the choice and treatment of subject are all implicated.

> From the foregoing it is obvious that the poetry of the instant present cannot have the same body or the same motion as the poetry of the before and after. It can never submit to the same conditions. It is never finished. There is no rhythm which returns upon itself, no serpent of eternity with its tail in its own mouth. There is no static perfection, none of that finality which we find so satisfying because we are so frightened. (*Complete Poems*, I, 184)

The 'seethe of mud', 'incipient putrescence' and 'the skies falling' *are* frightening things, and we therefore look to art in its wholeness and beauty for reassurance and satisfaction. But for Lawrence this is evasion of what life is all about – it is 'ignoring . . . the vast darkness that wheeled round about, with half-revealed shapes lurking on the edge' (*Rainbow*, pp. 437–8). The only poetry that can acknowledge the 'half-revealed shapes' is 'the rare new poetry'. It arises from 'the insurgent naked throb of the instant moment' and its 'utterance is like a spasm, naked contact with all influences at once'. It has neither 'goal' nor 'Inish': 'It does not want to get anywhere. It just takes place.' (*Complete Poems*, I, 185) And this is free verse.

> Much has been written about free verse. But all that can be said, first and last, is that free verse is, or should be, direct utterance from the instant, whole man. It is the soul and the mind and body surging at once, nothing left out. They speak all together. There is some confusion, some discord. But the confusion and the discord only belong to the reality as noise belongs to the plunge of water. It is no use inventing fancy

laws for free verse, no use drawing a melodic line which all the feet must toe. Free verse toes no melodic line, no matter what drill-sergeant. . . . All the laws we invent or discover . . . will fail to apply to free verse. They will only apply to some form of restricted, limited unfree verse. (*Complete Poems*, I, 184)

'Bavarian Gentians', which Lawrence wrote towards the end of 1929, a few months before he died, is far more disruptive of normal English than a poem like 'Bei Hennef', because the scale of subject being dealt with in 'Bavarian Gentians' is far broader. Whereas 'Bei Hennef' was written from an emotional situation that arose from Lawrence's finding himself in Europe with Frieda, and its references and strategies are specific, therefore, to a time and a place, 'Bavarian Gentians', while written with the specific prospect of death before him, is a poem that expands so far from the specific situation that individual emotion is subsumed into 'the forever incalculable journey of creation'. This makes for a complex poem, both in respect of the ideas Lawrence is handling, and of the language necessary to do justice to 'the confusion and the discord' of emotional reality. And yet the basic structure of the poem is surprisingly simple, and follows the three basic English sentence types: statement (or declarative sentence), question (interrogative sentence), and command (imperative sentence). The opening sentence is particularly straightforward:

Not every man has gentians in his house
in soft September, at slow, sad Michaelmas.
(*Complete Poems*, II, 975)

This is not unlike the language of the opening of 'Bei Hennef', and we find the characteristic reliance on patterns of sound for rhythm and mood: the twin 's' sounds of 'gentians' brought out by the secondary alliteration of 's' in 'his house', and especially by the dominant sounds of 'soft September, . . . slow, sad'; the parallel structures of 'in . . . ' 'in . . . '; the simple alliteration of 'man . . . Michaelmas'. We also find a straightforward pattern of dependent adjectival phrases after the main clause, telling where and when the gentians are, or are not, had: 'in his house', 'in soft September', 'at slow, sad Michaelmas'. Each of these three phrases could stand alone in relation to the main clause, so the relationship between them is one of co-ordination. They do not depend on each other in order to make sense within the sentence. But in so far as they play a part in the sound patterns of the verse, of course, they do in fact depend on each other, just as the main clause depends on them for the impact of its own sound patterns. We see, in other words, a syntactic ordering that gives us an understanding of the sentence, but we also hear certain sounds that work in a pattern that is capable of cutting across that ordering.

As the poem progresses the patterns of sound become more and more prominent. We also begin to realise that we cannot depend on the logical ordering of the syntax to present to us the meaning of the poem. To this extent, the opening has been misleading. The subsequent lines of the first verse are also declarative, but it soon becomes hard to tell just what is being declared.

> Bavarian gentians, tall and dark, but dark
> darkening the daytime torch-like with the smoking blueness
>   of Pluto's gloom,
> ribbed hellish flowers erect, with their blaze of darkness
>   spread blue,
> blown flat into points, by the heavy white draught of the
>   day.

The syntactical ordering ceases to be reliable, for the sentence, in spite of its length, is not a true sentence. It lacks a main verb. This part of the verse is actually made up of a string of subordinate phrases and clauses, some of which are directly dependent on the nominal group 'Bavarian gentians' – 'tall and dark', for example, and 'ribbed hellish flowers erect'. Others, however, relate to other subordinate phrases. So, 'with their blaze . . . ' depends upon 'ribbed hellish flowers erect', while 'by the heavy . . . ' relates equally to the two past participles 'spread' and 'blown'. The reader, after the comparative simplicity of the first sentence, spends much of the second expecting an equally simple grammatical resolution, but this expectation is finally overburdened by the weight of dependency that accumulates as the resolution is delayed longer and longer, and never arrives.

Instead, the patterns of sound begun in the first lines of the verse are multiplied to the extent that they threaten the coherence of what grammatical sense there is. The most obvious of these patterns is again repetition: 'dark, but dark/darkening', 'blueness . . . blue'. (This develops in the third verse into 'blue-smoking darkness,/Pluto's dark-blue blaze'.) But there is also alliteration, and the repetition both of verbal forms (the present participle, 'darkening', 'smoking', and the past participle, 'spread', 'blown') and of the structure of phrases ('blaze of darkness', 'draught of the day'). The overall impact of these patterns is one of intense compression. What is being declared is not to be understood in the straightforward logical structure of a traditional English sentence. Rather, we are being presented with a complex of sensations and ideas, of colour, of light and dark, of death, of sex, of pain, of all the associations released in the poet by the gentians. This process takes place in words and phrases that fit alongside one another not because they are intended to mean in a preordained logic but because they come together in this 'rapid momentaneous association of things'. It is as if the poet himself has no real control over language that is uttered 'from the instant'. As in the fifth verse of 'Bei Hennef', the structure of the individual's language comes under pressure, is in danger of proving inadequate, when faced with new or insufficiently understood emotion.

There has been some preparation for this in the first sentence, with the compression achieved in the two nominal groups 'soft September' and 'slow, sad Michaelmas'. The alliteration, by drawing attention to the rhythm, disguises the fact that the modifiers used here are unusual ones to find with these particular headwords. They are dictated not by common expectation but rather by the emotional needs of the poet. But the unexpected is far more striking in the language of the lines that complete the verse. Again, we find nominal groups that are packed with strange combinations of modifiers, headwords and qualifiers: 'ribbed hellish flowers erect' (modifier, modifier, headword, qualifier – but a qualifier that would be more normally expected in the position of a modifier); 'The heavy white draught' (determiner, modifier, modifier, headword). And we find, too, equally unusual combinations of verbal and adverbial groups. In 'dark/darkening the daytime torch-like', the verbal form is the present participle 'darkening', but the adverbial group is 'torch-like'. The combination captures precisely the ambiguity that Lawrence is exploring by which something intensely dark can actually enlighten new or buried emotions – here, the anticipation of death.

The second verse begins as if it is to repeat the declarative sentence structure of the first. The opening phrase, 'Torch-flowers of the blue-smoking darkness', is in fact another way of saying 'Bavarian gentians', and its position at the head of the verse makes the string of phrases that follows look as though this verse too will fail to resolve into a formal sentence. We recognise the by now familiar patterns of sound and compression: the alliteration of 'blue/blaze/black'; unusual combinations like 'black lamps' and 'giving off darkness'; the present participles, 'smoking' and 'giving', instead of a main verb. And there is a new element to be found in the use of compound words: 'Torch-flowers', 'blue-smoking', 'dark-blue', 'yellow-pale'. These create further compression, as if the poet is attempting to pack more meaning than is normally possible into the syntactic spaces of English grammar.

The real surprise in the verse, however, is when the last line transforms the whole sentence into a question: 'Whom have you come for, here in the white-cast day?' The grammar of the verse has to be realigned. What promised to be a string of phrases held together by patterns of dependency and co-ordination, but going nowhere, in the pattern developed in verse one, was actually a direct address by the poet to the 'Torch-flowers'. The items that had seemed to dominate the sentence were only preparations for its main clause – the main clause that the reader had assumed was not coming. The point here is not only that Lawrence has been refusing his reader the luxury of being able to predict where the poem is going. He has also been covertly biasing his grammar in the direction of the intensely personal. We have had the deliberately low-key opening to the poem and the striking description of verses one and (apparently) two – so striking that what is described seems to over-run the personality of the poet himself and his capacity to exercise control over his own language. But these are instantly undermined by the personal address, 'Whom have you come for', and by the implied answer, bringing out, as it does, the submerged assumption of line one that the poet *is* 'Not every man'. 'Not every man' may be a negative way for the poet to say 'me', but the denial of self of the first verse has been necessary for the establishing of those patterns of language that

have apparently threatened to overwhelm his individuality. Only
by the end of the second verse is he able to form the unaccustomed
grammar into a sentence that can express a personal inquiry.

Hereafter, the poet adopts the first person for the imperative
sentences that conclude the poem:

Reach me a gentian, give me a torch!
let me guide myself with the blue, forked torch of a flower
down the darker and darker stairs. . . .

Give me a flower on a tall stem, and three dark flames,
for I will go to the wedding, and be a wedding-guest
at the marriage of the living dark.

These final two verses are densely packed and the grammar
of verse three in particular demands concentrated attention from
the reader. Linguistic items, such as the word 'down' ('down the
darker and darker stairs', 'down the way Persephone goes'), and
familiar or everyday phrases and images ('just now, in first-frosted
September'), shed some light in the enveloping compression of
the syntax. The marriage of Persephone to Pluto, which takes
place *in* the dark and also represents a taking over by darkness,
is necessarily the focal centre of compression: she is taken

                                        as a bride
a gloom invisible enfolded in the deeper dark
of the arms of Pluto as he ravishes her once again
and pierces her once more with his passion of the utter
    dark

These lines are full of grammatical pitfalls that threaten the reader
with meaninglessness. The nominal group 'a gloom invisible', for
example, must be identified as a phrase in co-ordination with 'a
bride' and therefore equally to be 'enfolded' by the arms of Pluto.
Lawrence is denying the light normally associated with the word
'bride', and yet attempting to distinguish in this darkness between
the 'deeper dark' of Pluto and the mere 'gloom invisible' of the
bride who has descended, like the poet, from the realms of day.
The phrase 'of the utter dark' primarily means that Pluto's passion
derives from the darkness, but must also carry the sense that his

bride is pierced, or impregnated, *with* darkness, with the quality that is completely opposite to her normal nature.

In so far as the poem is dealing with the exploration of a personal realm of emotion, the acknowledged presence of 'me' and 'I' in these last verses clarifies the intention of the poet and acts as a reassurance that in the struggle for language, the struggle between chaos and control, the skill and responsibility of the writer have come through. He has been able, ultimately, to take the linguistic authority for describing his own death. His anticipation of death has indeed been subsumed into the cyclical patterns of life and death, light and dark, but in a way that is capable of enhancing and validating individual extinction. In the shorter version of the poem, which for a long time was regarded as the authoritative text, this validation is missing, for the poem ends:

> . . . pierced with the passion of dense gloom,
> among the splendour of torches of darkness, shedding
> darkness on the lost bride and her groom.
>
> (*Complete Poems*, II, 697)

The absence of the final verse makes the poet into a shadowy voyeur, instead of a guest whose presence, at the moment of personal extinction, honours and supports the association in matrimony of those principles vital to 'the journey of creation'.

In the essay 'Life', possibly written as early as 1916,[6] Lawrence had also anticipated the moment of death.

> And do I fear the invisible dark hand of death plucking me into the darkness, gathering me blossom by blossom from the stem of life into the unknown of my afterwards? I fear it only in reverence and with strange satisfaction, to be gathered blossom by blossom, all my life long, into the finality of the unknown which is my end. (*Phoenix*, p. 698)

Here, too, we find the celebration, the honour, that in 'Bavarian Gentians' is transformed into the role of 'wedding-guest'. The difference, though, between an essay written by a man in his early thirties and a poem composed during periods of illness a few months before his death is caught in the change from the perspective of 'all my life long' to the immediacy of 'let me guide myself'. In 'Bavarian Gentians', in its patterns of compression and claustrophobia, and in the emerging sense of self that can shape this gloom into question and command, we find the kind of 'direct utterance from the instant' that, for Lawrence, is a crucial feature of the language of poetry.

Personality, as I suggested in Chapter 1, was always a characteristic of Lawrence's writing, and was responsible for the vitality and distinctiveness of his work in both poetry and prose. His handling of language through the medium of various literary forms demonstrates his ability to suspend personality in the interests of art, as well as to draw life from it, and sometimes to indulge it. His work will always be read as peculiarly his own, as uniquely 'Lawrentian', but the close examination of his language reveals something of the means by which that uniqueness was achieved and the integrity with which it was pursued.

Notes

CHAPTER 1

1. Michael Bell (ed.), *The Context of English Literature: 1900–1930* (London: Methuen, 1980), p. 70.

2. F. R. Leavis, *D.H. Lawrence, Novelist* (London: Chatto and Windus, 1955), p. 152. Leavis' point, however, is that Birkin serves a vital role in the novel, enabling Lawrence to enact a 'testing and exploring of the conscious and formulated conclusions that Birkin thinks he has settled in securely enough to act upon' (p. 176).

3. I allow letters as a form not because I regard them as *literary* forms in the sense that a novel is a literary form, but for the simple reason that they constitute a form of written expression with its own distinctive features, including the opportunities afforded by writing for a single known reader.

4. In traditional grammar, a 'complement' *completes* a sentence in which the main verb is one of being, seeing, becoming, feeling, etc – 'The cat is black', 'The woman feels sad'. It is distinguished from an 'object', which is the item on which the action of the sentence is performed – 'He kicked the cat'. In systemic linguistics, however, the 'complement' is 'the part of a sentence which answers the question "Who or what? . . . *after* the verb' (Margaret Berry, *An Introduction to Systemic Linguistics: Volume 1, Structures and Systems* (London: Batsford, 1975), p. 64). See also Norman Blake, *Traditional English Grammar and Beyond* (London: Macmillan, 1988). Chapter 4 below deals with some of the terminology and analytical methods of systemic linguistics.

5. James Joyce, *A Portrait of the Artist as a Young Man* (Harmondsworth: Penguin, 1962 edn), p. 221.

6. Henry James, *The Portrait of a Lady* (Harmondsworth: Penguin, 1963 edn), p. xiii.

7. T.S. Eliot, 'East Coker', 11.68–71, *The Four Quartets* (London: Faber and Faber, 1944).

8. T.S. Eliot, 'The Dry Salvages', 1.93, *The Four Quartets*.

9. Eliot, 'The Dry Salvages', 11.212–13.

10. Jacob Korg, *Language in Modern Literature: Innovation and Experiment* (Brighton: Harvester, 1979), p. 6.

11. Korg, p. 6.

12. T.S. Eliot, 'The Burial of the Dead', 1.22, *The Waste Land;*
The Hollow Men, 1.23; in *The Complete Poems and Plays of T.S. Eliot*
(London: Faber and Faber, 1969).

13. Korg, p. 3.

14. Bell, p. 51. Bell, in one of the best recent introductions to
Modernism, has been comparing a sentence from the 'Oxen of the
Sun' episode of *Ulysses* with the final sentence of *Sons and Lovers*.
See Chapter 7 in this book for discussion of Lawrence's treatment of
language as a major theme of a fictional work in *The Rainbow*.

15. Octavio Paz, *Children of the Mire*, tr. R. Phillips (Cambridge,
Mass.: Harvard University Press, 1974), p. 148, cited by Korg, p. 28.

16. Bell, p. 69.

CHAPTER 2

1. Ford Madox Ford, *Return to Yesterday* (New York: Liveright,
1932) pp. 376–8, in Edward Nehls, *D.H. Lawrence: A Composite
Biography: Volume 1: 1885–1919* (Madison, Wisconsin: University of
Wisconsin Press, 1957), pp. 151–2.

2. Nehls, p. 558 n.124; Harry T. Moore, *The Priest of Love: A
Life of D.H. Lawrence* (Harmondsworth: Penguin, 1976 edn), p. 107.
Subsequent references to Nehls are included in the text.

3. Emile Delavenay, *D.H. Lawrence: The Man and His Work:
The Formative Years, 1885–1919*, tr. Katharine M. Delavenay (London:
Heinemann, 1972), p. 11. Subsequent references are included in the text.

4. Keith Sagar draws attention to this example in *D.H. Lawrence:
Life Into Art* (Harmondsworth: Viking, 1985), p. 81.

5. Jessie Chambers ('E.T.'), *D.H. Lawrence: A Personal Record*
(London: Cass, 1965, 2nd edn), pp. 92–4. Subsequent references are
included in the text.

6. We should, however, bear in mind that these early observations
will have been coloured by Jessie's later opinions of Mrs Lawrence (for
example pp. 201–2).

7. Rose Marie Burwell, 'A Checklist of Lawrence's Reading'
in Keith Sagar (ed.), *A D.H. Lawrence Handbook* (Manchester:
Manchester University Press, 1982), pp. 66–70.

8. Sagar, *Life Into Art*, pp. 17–18.

9. The Cambridge edition reads (among other changes) 'grey descendants' and 'reeds' for 'weeds' (p. 3).

10. See also Keith Sagar, *D.H. Lawrence: A Calendar of His Works*
(Manchester: Manchester University Press, 1979), p. 23.

11. Keith Sagar, *The Life of D.H. Lawrence* (London: Methuen,
1980), p. 51.

12. Mark Schorer (ed.), '*Paul Morel*: A Facsimile of Six Fragments'
in *D.H. Lawrence: 'Sons and Lovers': A Facsimile of the Manuscript*
(Berkeley, California, and London: University of California Press, 1977),

pp. 33–5. 'Tunns' is unclear in the manuscript, and 'dirt, without' is an incomplete sentence.

13. Schorer (ed.) *'Sons and Lovers*: A Facsimile of the Manuscript', in *D.H. Lawrence: 'Sons and Lovers': A Facsimile of the Manuscript*, pp. 32–3.

14. Schorer, 'Introduction', pp. 8–9.

CHAPTER 3

1. Sagar, *Life Into Art*, p. 192.

2. John Worthen, *D.H. Lawrence and the Idea of the Novel* (London: Macmillan, 1979), p. 79.

3. See Sagar, *Calendar*, pp. 144–5 for details of dating.

4. See Sagar, *Calendar*, pp. 8–9 for discussion of precise dating.

5. Sagar, *Life Into Art*, p. 137, citing Lawrence's *Fantasia of the Unconscious and Psychoanalysis and the Unconscious* (Harmondsworth: Penguin, 1971), p. 15.

6. Worthen, p. 61.

CHAPTER 4

1. See Berry for a full account of the terms and methods employed in systemic linguistics.

2. T.S. Eliot, *The Hollow Men*, 11.72–6.

CHAPTER 5

1. Sagar, *Life Into Art*, p. 267ff makes this point in more detail.

2. See David Gerard, 'A Glossary of Nottinghamshire Dialect and Mining Terms' in Sagar, *Handbook*, p. 176.

3. Gerard, p. 171.

4. See, for example, Dick Leith, *A Social History of English* (London: Routledge and Kegan Paul, 1973), Chapter 5, especially Parts 1 and 2, for wide-ranging discussion of the issues touched upon here.

CHAPTER 6

1. Jane Austen, *Mansfield Park* (Harmondsworth: Penguin, 1966 edn), p. 51; George Eliot, *Middlemarch* (Harmondsworth: Penguin, 1965 edn), p. 32; Thomas Hardy, *The Mayor of Casterbridge* (London: Macmillan, 1965 edn), p. 30.

CHAPTER 7

1. Gerard, p. 167.

CHAPTER 8

1. See Chambers, pp. 61–2, 94–5, 99ff, 114–15.
2. Christopher Hassall, *A Biography of Edward Marsh* (New York: Harcourt, Brace and Co., 1959), pp. 193–4.
3. Hassall, p. 322.
4. Edward Marsh, *A Number of People* (New York and London: Harper, 1939), p. 234.
5. It is hardly necessary to add that Lawrence's views, as summarised here, beg an enormous number of questions, some of which have been tackled by critics engaged in the debates of the last twenty years over what literature is, what it should be doing, and how it should be doing it.
6. See Sagar, *Calendar*, p. 72.

Select Bibliography

WORKS BY D.H. LAWRENCE DISCUSSED OR DRAWN ON FOR ANALYSIS

Fiction

'The Captain's Doll', in *Three Novellas* (Harmondsworth: Penguin, 1960).
'England, My England', in *England, My England* (Harmondsworth: Penguin, 1960).
'Love Among the Haystacks', in *Love Among the Haystacks and Other Stories* (Harmondsworth: Penguin, 1960).
'The Man Who Loved Islands', in *Love Among the Haystacks and Other Stories* (Harmondsworth: Penguin, 1960).
'*Paul Morel*: A Facsimile of Six Fragments', in Mark Schorer (ed.), *D.H. Lawrence: 'Sons and Lovers': A Facsimile of the Manuscript* (Berkeley, California, and London: University of California Press, 1977).
The Plumed Serpent (Harmondsworth: Penguin, 1950).
The Rainbow (Harmondsworth: Penguin, 1949).
St Mawr, in *St Mawr and The Virgin and the Gipsy* (Harmondsworth: Penguin, 1950).
Sons and Lovers (Harmondsworth: Penguin, 1948).
'*Sons and Lovers*: A Facsimile of the Manuscript', in Mark Schorer (ed.), *D.H. Lawrence: 'Sons and Lovers': A Facsimile of the Manuscript* (Berkeley, California, and London: University of California Press, 1977).
The Virgin and the Gipsy, in *St Mawr and The Virgin and the Gipsy* (Harmondsworth: Penguin, 1950).
The White Peacock (Harmondsworth: Penguin, 1950).
Women in Love (Harmondsworth: Penguin, 1960).
'You Touched Me', in *England, My England* (Harmondsworth: Penguin, 1960).

Poetry

'Bavarian Gentians', in *Complete Poems*, vol II.
'Bei Hennef', in *Complete Poems*, vol I.
The Complete Poems of D.H. Lawrence, ed. Vivian de Sola Pinto and Warren Roberts, 2 vols (London: Heinemann, 1972 edn).

'Snap-Dragon', in *Complete Poems*, vol I.
'Sunday Afternoon in Italy', in *Complete Poems*, vol I.
'A Young Wife', in *Complete Poems*, vol I.

Essays and Other Writings

'Art and Morality', in *Phoenix*.
'Art and the Individual', in *Phoenix II*.
'Autobiographical Sketch', in *Phoenix II*.
Fantasia of the Unconscious and Psychoanalysis and the Unconscious (Harmondsworth: Penguin, 1971).
'Foreword to *Collected Poems*', in *Complete Poems*, vol I.
'Foreword to *Pansies*', in *Complete Poems*, vol I.
'Foreword to *Women in Love*', in *Phoenix II*.
'Hymns in a Man's Life', in *Phoenix II*.
The Letters of D.H. Lawrence: Volume I: 1901–13, ed. James T. Boulton (Cambridge: Cambridge University Press, 1979).
The Letters of D.H. Lawrence: Volume II: 1913–16, ed. George Zytaruk and James T. Boulton (Cambridge: Cambridge University Press, 1981).
The Letters of D.H. Lawrence; Volume III: 1916–21, ed. James T. Boulton and Andrew Robertson (Cambridge: Cambridge University Press, 1984).
'Life', in *Phoenix*.
'Morality and the Novel', in *Phoenix*.
'The Novel', in *Phoenix II*.
'The Novel and the Feelings', in *Phoenix*.
Phoenix: The Posthumous Papers of D.H. Lawrence, ed. Edward D. McDonald (London: Heinemann, 1936).
Phoenix II: Uncollected, Unpublished and Other Prose Works by D.H. Lawrence, ed. Warren Roberts and Harry T. Moore (London: Heinemann, 1968).
'Poetry of the Present', in *Complete Poems*, vol I.
'Preface to *Collected Poems*, in *Complete Poems*, vol I.
'Study of Thomas Hardy', in *Phoenix*.
'Surgery for the Novel – or a Bomb', in *Phoenix*.
Twilight in Italy (Harmondsworth: Penguin, 1960)
'Why the Novel Matters', in *Phoenix*.

OTHER SELECTED WORKS

BELL, MICHAEL (ed.), *The Context of English Literature: 1900–1930* (London: Methuen, 1980).
BERRY, MARGARET, *An Introduction to Systemic Linguistics: Volume 1, Structures and Systems* (London: Batsford, 1975).

CHAMBERS, JESSIE ('E.T.'), *D.H. Lawrence: A Personal Record* (London: Cass, 1965, 2nd edn).

DELAVENAY, EMILE, *D.H. Lawrence: The Man and His Work: The Formative Years, 1885–1919*, tr. Katharine M. Delavenay (London: Heinemann, 1972).

KORG, JACOB, *Language in Modern Literature: Innovation and Experiment* (Brighton: Harvester, 1979).

LEAVIS, F. R., *D.H. Lawrence, Novelist* (London: Chatto and Windus, 1955).

LEITH, DICK, *A Social History of English* (London: Routledge and Kegan Paul, 1973).

MOORE, HARRY T., *The Priest of Love: A Life of D.H. Lawrence* (Harmondsworth: Penguin, 1976 edn).

NEHLS, EDWARD, *D.H. Lawrence: A Composite Biography: Volume 1: 1885–1919* (Madison, Wisconsin: University of Wisconsin Press, 1957).

SAGAR, KEITH, *D.H. Lawrence: A Calendar of His Works* (Manchester: Manchester University Press, 1979).

SAGAR, KEITH, *A D.H. Lawrence Handbook* (Manchester: Manchester University Press, 1982).

SAGAR, KEITH, *D.H. Lawrence: Life Into Art* (Harmondsworth: Viking, 1985).

SAGAR, KEITH, *The Life of D.H. Lawrence* (London: Methuen, 1980).

WORTHEN, JOHN, *D.H. Lawrence and the Idea of the Novel* (London: Macmillan, 1979).

Index